Roger & Gayle

To a great couple ♡

Kaye Eisenhower Morgan

How Being a Niece of
President Eisenhower impacted my life

KAYE EISENHOWER MORGAN

WestBow Press books may be ordered through booksellers or by contacting:

WestBow Press
A Division of Thomas Nelson & Zondervan
1663 Liberty Drive
Bloomington, IN 47403
www.westbowpress.com
1 (866) 928-1240

ISBN: 978-1-4908-8504-9 (sc)
ISBN: 978-1-4908-8506-3 (hc)
ISBN: 978-1-4908-8505-6 (e)

Library of Congress Control Number: 2015909737

Print information available on the last page.

WestBow Press rev. date: 08/12/2015

ALSO BY THE AUTHOR, Kaye Eisenhower Morgan:

The Eisenhower Legacy
A Tribute to Ida Stover Eisenhower and David Jacob Eisenhower
First Edition published April 2010
By Roesler Enterprises Publishing

Contents

DEDICATION

This book is dedicated to my parents
and to all the descendants
of Ida and David Eisenhower

Preface

As an Eisenhower, growing up in the 1930s, and 1940s, I had a very interesting life. As I related some of my experiences to friends, they would always say, “Kaye, you’ve got to write a book.”

So many things happened because I was an Eisenhower; many things happened because life is what it is. No one escapes without some joy, some heartbreak, and no family is perfect. Every family has some dysfunction of some kind, and we must learn to forgive although we can’t erase our memory completely, the forgiveness must be complete.

As a teenager, I got the message, “Kaye, your purpose in this life is to love without being loved in return.” That’s a powerful message!

After living with an alcoholic mother, an alcoholic husband, and four children, two of whom had their special problems, I’m surprised I’ve lived this long. So many times I wanted to lock myself in a closet and make the world go away, but the world of problems called and I answered.

I also determined that the Eisenhower fame would not affect who I was. I had seen too many people changed by the spotlight of fame, and it was not pretty. I determined to be down to earth, to be myself, come what may. Even Uncle Ike, who became the highest-ranking person in this country, if not the world, never stood on protocol within the confines of family and friends. He was as down to earth as anyone I've ever known, as were all his brothers. I am very fortunate to have known them.

Introduction

Life was so different in the 1930s. Growing up in southwestern Pennsylvania, all family members – cousins, grandparents, aunts, uncles, etc. lived close to each other. Visiting grandparents or family on weekends was a short drive or a short streetcar ride. I had no grandparents; my mother was orphaned as a young child, and my Dad's parents lived far away in Abilene, Kansas. Mother's two sisters and a brother did not live nearby. All Dad's brothers lived far away – Tacoma, Washington; Mission Hills, Kansas; Topeka, Kansas; and Junction City, Kansas. Uncle Ike moved according to where the Army sent him. Consequently, our family had no "family" get-togethers" on Sundays as other families did.

My life was turned upside down in the 1940s and 1950s because I was a niece of General and President Eisenhower when the name Eisenhower was truly magic. No matter where Dwight Eisenhower went, overflow crowds were sure to follow, much of what happened to George Washington when the Revolutionary War was over.

Unwanted fame followed me wherever I went because I was an Eisenhower. Even after I married, and my name became Morgan, the fame continued to follow me.

In my college years, marriage, and moves around the country to Roscoe, Illinois, La Grange, Illinois, Houston, Tucson, Phoenix, Cincinnati, it never quit.

In between bouts of fame and journalists, much of my life was quite mundane, but sprinkled with exciting events that I love to relate. I was Apple Blossom Queen (Queen Shenandoah XXVI), Cotton Queen, a 4-H leader and music director, and a youth counselor. I served Mobile Meals in Tucson, was a church organist and children's choir director in Roscoe, Illinois and a Sunday School teacher and church Deacon in Tucson. I served as a teacher in the Blind Center in Tucson, and a counselor in the Juvenile Division of Superior Court in Pima County, Arizona. In Mesa, Arizona I was a church Deacon, president of our local computer club, president of our local writers club, Regent of our DAR chapter and Day Captain at the Desert Botanical Garden in Phoenix. These were all exciting things that I did.

Over the years, I made many trips to Abilene, Kansas, and our family reunions, which were quite spectacular.

Finally, I made trips to Gettysburg, Uncle Ike and Aunt Mamie's only home they ever owned. I got to see the first three homes in Gettysburg where they lived when Uncle Ike was stationed there sometime in the 1920s.

Seeing the World War II Memorial in Washington D.C. was overwhelming, knowing my uncle was responsible for directing the greatest army ever assembled. This memorial honors his efforts.

As a kid, I couldn't figure out why Mother didn't want me around. I loved her so much and just wanted her attention and love. Kids learn to live with whatever situation. Many years later I vowed that if and when I had children, they would NOT be treated as I was. I vowed I would listen to them, care for them and show them they were loved, come what may.

I remember my first trip to Abilene so vividly though I was only four years old. The trip to Abilene, Kansas for the 1945 Homecoming Gala was something to remember! The trip to Washington DC for the 1953 Inauguration was spectacular and memorable. Many trips to Abilene, Gettysburg and Washington DC in the future always featured Dwight D. Eisenhower. Visiting the World War II

Memorial shows General Dwight D. Eisenhower as a focal point of the European Theater of Operations. Seeing the World War II Memorial was an emotional experience for me. My trips to Europe had Dwight Eisenhower or his ancestors prominently displayed in places.

There were six Eisenhower brothers who grew to maturity, all of whom became the tops in their chosen profession. Arthur was a banker and head of the Kansas City Board of Trade. Edgar was a famous lawyer, more famous for his golf playing up and down the west coast. Dwight was the third son. Roy owned his own pharmacy in Junction City, Kansas (he died young at 49 of a stroke in 1942 just months before his father died). My Dad was chief electrical engineer for the West Penn Power Company, based in Charleroi, Pennsylvania. Milton was a famous educator (he was head of Kansas State, Penn State, and Johns Hopkins) and unofficial ambassador for Uncle Ike during his presidency.

I got to know my uncles, something most of my cousins were not able to do. Each of the brothers was special in his way. I am so lucky and grateful that I got to know each and every one of them, except for Roy. I remember seeing him in Junction City in 1938, but the memory is vague.

Because we were Eisenhowers, naturally we followed Uncle Ike's career through the army, to Columbia, to NATO and through the Presidency. In order to become President, he had to give up his commission in the army. Once his Presidency was over, he reclaimed his army title.

I got to go places, meet people and see things that most people my age could not dream of. This was the 1940s and 1950s when women were primarily homebodies.

I am now the last remaining of my generation of this Eisenhower family. There are many other Eisenhower (Isenhauer, Icenhauer, Izenhauer, etc.) families in the country, most of whom trace their lineage back to my ancestor, the original Hans Nicholas Eisenhauer who first migrated to this country.

I must caution the reader that everyone has their memories – When my brother and I would look back over the years, he would remember some things; I would remember other things. In going places with my children and grandchildren, they each see events from different perspectives. So, here, I try to relate events and my experiences. It was my life, none other. Sometimes I will remember something, but can't place it in time or place. Then, I must go through journals and scrapbooks in an effort to "pin down" that piece of memory. Memory will play tricks on me. I eliminated events that seem amorphous, blurry or that I can't place.

Another important thing is "where we are from." Our answer typically is the place of our birth. My perspective is that I am from a good family who taught me all the right things, respected me as a person, made sure I got religious and secular education and rigidly disciplined me. I learned early to do things the right way, and that short cuts are not productive.

When I was growing up, we did not have birthday parties. Mother explained to me that most of the families in the area were poor. Mother and Dad did not want kids coming to a birthday party, expecting to bring gifts they could ill afford. Our celebration of birthdays was cake and ice cream after dinner. When dinner was over, Mother would bring forth her wonderful cake, and then were we told we could canvass the neighborhood and invite all who wanted to come for cake and ice cream. That way, no one was expected to bring gifts.

Another Eisenhower custom was that Buddy and I did not get a great amount of praise. A couple of times when I did something I thought was spectacular and would surely elicit praise and a pat on the back, so to speak, Dad just looked at me and said, "That's what you are supposed to do."

We are all from a different perspective, different families. Even the poorest and most disadvantaged can rise to greatness, as the Eisenhowers did. The times of our lives produce different perspectives. Some will do well in spite of their family or social environments. Some will succumb to their bad environment. Everyone is different.

Society, technology, and other changes impact our lives differently. I grew up in a different era. We had no computers, TV, cell phones (in fact, not everyone had a phone), no GPS devices (we needed good maps then), no electronic gadgets at all. If you lived in a rural area, even electricity was limited. Most people did have a radio. People gathered around the radio to listen to the six o'clock news. Newspapers were common though not everyone could afford a subscription. Cars were scarce. We could ride our bikes in the middle of the highway in front of our house with no fear of traffic at times.

Cars did not have automatic transmissions. They were just being developed for cars about the time I was in high school, and only the high-end cars had the first automatic transmissions.

I learned to drive a humpback 1941 Ford. Manipulating the clutch and brake on the steep Pennsylvania hills was tricky and took some practice to get right. Also parallel parking. Small towns with their narrow streets necessitated such parking, and we had to maneuver correctly on the first turn. The constant clutching on changing gears was something to learn quickly. Clutch in – shift gears – clutch out slowly – clutch in – shift gears – clutch out slowly. No way I could do that anymore.

Nowadays we would look back on that era as a permanent camping trip. I came from this time. My hindsight view of many decades gives me a different perspective than those much younger.

I also realize that events that impact our early lives can have great influence on our later lives, that one event will send you one direction, and your life takes off from there..

In my trip through this life, I've been in every state in the union in the contiguous 48. I've seen most of the National Parks and many state parks. I've been in all the major cities except New York City and Salt Lake City and a good many of the smaller cities and towns throughout this great country.

Along the way I've incurred almost every human agony, endured much, but learned love, tolerance and love of God and His people. I also got to know all my uncles. They were truly the greatest people I've ever known -- all of them. I was so fortunate to have known all of the Eisenhower brothers – Arthur, Edgar, Dwight, Roy, Earl (my father) and Milton.

I was so privileged to have a father like mine. He was so very strict, but fun loving; his greatest joys were (1) gardening and (2) taking us kids on Sunday drives into the mountains. He had a temper and would paddle first and ask questions later. He had the patience of Job, especially when teaching me. I was a slow learner, not dumb, just slow. It took me a while to learn to tie my shoes. What a struggle that was, but he stuck with it, and I finally learned. In first grade when we tackled arithmetic for the first time, I was so lost and confused, but Dad spent his evenings with me teaching me the wonders of mathematics. (he was the expert, being an electrical engineer). The wizardry of math finally made it into my brain, and the light bulb went on. Since then I've been a whiz at math. I've always appreciated his patience with me.

I was privileged also to have a mother such as mine. She grew up in an elegant home, with upstairs and downstairs servants, kitchen maids and gardeners and coachmen on their carriage (until they got a car). Because of her upbringing, Mother could pound proper etiquette into us tone-deaf kids. She also taught Dad some proper manners, a funny story. Even though she was an alcoholic, she did not shirk her duties as wife and mother. Our house was spotless, and always welcoming to whoever showed up. We kids were also spotless as she could make us. One day she got me all dolled up in my best finery for some occasion (that escapes me), and I promptly went outside to play. I was filthy, and Mother was furious!

This is my story, none other.

ABILENE, KANSAS 1938
My First of Many Travels

The bright-yellow wheat, ripening in the summer sun, billowed in waves across the flat land. Having experienced only southwestern Pennsylvania, a land of heavily forested rolling hills, with many streams, creeks, rivers and lakes, this flat land was foreign to my four-year-old eyes. The yellow land was as flat as a table top for miles and miles, and there were so few houses and miles apart. I had never seen such a world!

We were traveling from North Charleroi, a small borough of about one thousand people south of Pittsburgh, to Abilene, Kansas, to visit my father's parents, David and Ida Eisenhower. Dad's brother, Dwight and his son Johnny would join us there. It would take us three days to get there, as there were no freeways, and the highways were simply two-lane concrete ribbons across the flat countryside. Nowadays Interstate 70 pretty much follows the route we took.

I don't remember where we stayed along the way. However, I do know that there was no such thing as a motel at that time, so we must have stayed in local hotels.

Entranced by such a different landscape, I held on tightly to the partially lowered rear window of our gray mid-1930s Ford Slantback, with my nose pressed to the window. My brother, Buddy, hung onto the other window, also mesmerized. We were so fascinated that neither of us would lie down for a nap. The memory is still vivid. What a trip!

Upon arriving in Abilene, we were greeted enthusiastically by Grandmother Ida and Grandfather David. They were always so happy to see their boys, since they all lived far away and did not get home to Abilene very often. Grandma Ida promptly took charge of us kids and would not let us out of her sight. Grandpa tried to get me to sit on his lap, but I was an explorer and didn't want to sit still. Grandpa and Grandma had seven boys (one had died as an infant) and no girls. So all their granddaughters got the same treatment: constant cuddling, lap sitting and favoritism!

My memories of that trip are very specific: the chicken run, the garage (which once was a barn), watermelons, Grandma's cat, the school and playground across the street, and the big beds we slept in upstairs. And Grandmother. Everyone adored her. All her sons talked of her as if she were a saint, but their father was seldom mentioned. Grandmother Ida was the huge influence in their lives. Grandfather David was a very taciturn person and was not given to much conversation as Grandma was.

While we were visiting Grandmother and Grandfather, Mother and Dad stayed in one bedroom upstairs and Buddy and I stayed in the other. These were the two bedrooms plus a small closet-size room, where once the six Eisenhower brothers slept, with my grandparents' bedroom downstairs. When their bedroom was upstairs, the newborns would be bedded in a dresser drawer. Later, an addition that was built for my grandfather's father, Jacob, was available after Jacob died.

Eventually, my grandparents added a bathroom in the addition to the house. No more running to the outhouse in all kinds of weather. Not fun, especially in the cold Kansas winters. Of course, that's what chamber pots were for in the middle of the nights.

Although Dwight and his son Johnny were also visiting, I truly don't remember them and don't know where they stayed.

Watermelon is a vivid memory. I had never seen or tasted watermelon before. It was paradise defined, as I had never tasted anything so divinely delicious! Buddy and I gnawed our way to the rind and didn't want to stop there. When the grownups took the rinds away from us, I acquiesced, but Buddy threw a fit. The rinds were then thrown to the chickens, who promptly devoured them. Buddy hung onto the chicken wire fencing, his nose poking through the screen, screaming at the chickens because they were eating *his* watermelon. I'll never forget that. I swear to this day that Kansas has the best watermelon in the world! And chickens agree!

Grandma was my favorite person. She was always there with us. She adored children and spent most of her time with us. She allowed us to cross the street to the school playground as she sat on the front porch diligently watching us. Sometimes she would call us home, either because it was dinnertime, or bullies had shown up. She explained that some kids were mean and that it wasn't appropriate for us to be around them.

Grandma's cat was something new to Buddy and me. We had never been around pets, much less a cat, and so we were fascinated by it. The poor thing was bedeviled by the two of us and soon took to hiding under the porch refusing to come out.

While we all were there, Dad, Dwight and Johnny, who was sixteen at the time, built a small cement patio onto the back of the house where it was shady and Grandpa and Grandma could sit and enjoy the day. It used to be quite muddy. Before the cement was dry, Dwight and Dad agreed that they should put their initials in the concrete, because, they said, "Someday Ed (one of their older brothers) will come by and claim he did this." That slab broke apart several years ago and now sits in the basement of the Eisenhower Museum in storage, for lack of anyplace else to put it.

My grandparents' home is now part of the Eisenhower Center in Abilene. The school is gone, and the property was purchased to become part of the Eisenhower Center complex. Added were several other structures – the museum, the library, the Place of Meditation (where Dwight, Mamie and their first son Doud Dwight are buried), pylons depicting the Eisenhower family, and a statue of Uncle Ike.

My traveling life began with this first trip. Many others would follow.

Grandma Ida with Kaye and Buddy 1938,
at the Eisenhower home in Abilene

My baby picture on the landing to the second floor bedroom area of the Eisenhower home. I was about 6 months old

Life in the 1930s and Early 1940s

While growing up in the 1930s and 1940s life was so incredibly different from today. People didn't have "stuff." Hoboes abounded, people were out of work, and few owned cars. Neighborhoods were quiet and people knew their neighbors. Everyone knew where he or she belonged. Life was, if not rigid, at least well ordered. There was a calm, and a sense of belonging, that imbued our culture. That feeling is gone now. I wish we could reclaim that once more.

I remember the 1930s vividly. So many men were out of work and women didn't generally work outside the home, unless they were secretaries, nurses or school teachers. Factories, and the mills across the river from us, were silent, but some larger mills had minimal activity. Life was terribly impacted not only by the Depression, but also by the millworker strikes that went on interminably. Whole families had literally no income at times.

Large Victorian homes and other two-storied homes were turned into multiple apartments. Homes were abandoned and left vacant. Some homes in our neighborhood became apartments, and doorways were altered to accommodate upstairs tenants. People shared what they had. Older folks who owned the larger homes must have had some kind of income, perhaps income from investments, I don't know. I just know that many of the people in those homes were not working. Consequently, few had cars, either.

Hoboes camped by the railroad tracks just down the weed-, rat-, and snake-infested hillside, between our home and the river. Several times a week, the hoboes would canvass our neighborhood. Mother would answer the knock on the door, see their plight, and invite them into our kitchen, where she sat them down at our kitchen table, and fixed them a meal and packed a sack lunch for them to take with them. We never feared the hoboes, as they were simply homeless men with no income. But many people on our street would have nothing to do with them. The men would beg what they could, and take it back to their camp by the tracks and most likely shared it with others. I never went down the hill to their encampment, but Buddy did.

People never locked their doors; in fact, they even left their car keys in the ignitions. It was nice to be able to trust our neighbors. We never locked our doors until one night Mother found a drunk sleeping on our front porch. Thereafter, our doors were locked.

Many people could not afford garbage service, so they threw their garbage down the embankment facing the streetcar tracks, which is why there were so many rats and snakes. We kids knew that the big snakes were good snakes that ate rats, so we left them alone.

Monongahela River (called "The Mon") from behind our house. The river is wide and deep. Thousands of tons of coal on river barges regularly made their way downstream to the mills near Pittsburgh. Factories and mills are across the river.

GUARD, MARYLAND

For children, Guard was a magical, idyllic place, filled with places to roam, hide, or hang out all day long with no fear of interfering adults or nosy neighbors. We could swim in the creek (which we pronounced 'crik' and I didn't know it was spelled 'creek' until I was a teenager) or the pool built by my father and the Driscoll sons, climb the mountain, investigate the woods, go into the old octagon-shaped church on the mountainside and play with the old pump organ, and then run through the small cemetery (we weren't afraid of tombstones). The pool still exists today, but the drainage system appears to be different, and is painted blue.

Guard was the property that Mother's foster father, J.J. Driscoll, had bought, probably in the early 1900s, from the Guard family (whose gravestones were in the small cemetery mentioned above). This land spread about a mile -- along stretch of mountain valley between what is now known as Confluence Lake and the main highway. Guard was a place, not really a town or village or anything like that, just a place. Confluence Lake was not there at that time; there was a little town of Summerfield. Summerfield was demolished and totally flooded when the dam and Confluence Lake was constructed. It is now a state park lake and camping site.

Everyone in southwest Pennsylvania knew James J. Driscoll, Manager of the Connellsville Courier, the newspaper started, owned and operated by Mother's father, Henry P. Snyder. Everyone knew Mr. Driscoll as "JJ." We kids called him Pop Driscoll or Grandpa Jim. But JJ was famous and well liked. After Henry Snyder and his wife died, leaving my mother an orphan, JJ became the President/CEO of the newspaper and the Guardian of Henry's four children.

JJ eventually took my mother into his home, after a series of mishaps with her family, and Mother became the 12th child in his large Catholic family.

In shaping the small community at Guard, Mom and Pop Driscoll first built what he and everyone called "the Big House," which they named Lonesome Pine. The large pine for which the place was named still exists. The house was a huge, two-story oversized summer place with plenty of sleeping spaces. The downstairs had a screened porch completely across the front with all kinds of porch furniture. The central room, which was a living-dining combination, was complete with an old grand piano, horsehair furniture, huge dining table, and lots of easy chairs, and an old Victrola. This room is where everyone retreated when the weather was bad and sitting on the screened porch would get you a bit wet.

The back of the house had a screened porch with trestle tables and benches for eating. We often had 50 or so people on weekends when much of the family – many of their 12 children and the grandchildren showed up. Buddy and I were considered their grandchildren. Meals were eaten in shifts, with the children eating first.

The entire upstairs was literally wall-to-wall beds, one huge dormitory with about a dozen beds. There was one, perhaps two, tiny bedrooms enclosed with a door, for adults only

The kitchen in the back of the house had a linoleum floor, an old icebox, which the Iceman would have to refill regularly, a double sink but no running water, and a coal stove. Years later, sometime in the 1940s a bathroom was added just off the kitchen. People would stand in line 10 deep waiting to take a "real" bath instead of going to the creek, which was ice cold the year round.

On the back porch, with wooden counter top, was the hand pump for water. It was the only water available and one had to prime it first. Woe to anyone who used the pump, then forgot to leave a bucket of water for the next person to use to prime the pump.

There was an icehouse out back, not far from the kitchen, down the path toward the outhouse. The icehouse would keep a lot of stuff that we nowadays would put in refrigerators – extra butter, milk, etc. Sometimes Mom Driscoll would send us kids down the road to the main highway where there was a little store about a half mile away, where we could buy eggs or milk as needed.

The outhouse, with three different size holes, was further down the path behind the Big House, built over a small creek, which eliminated the need for cleaning out a cesspool.

As the Driscoll children married, some built their cabins along the road on either side of the Big House or Lonesome Pine. To my remembrance, there were six or so cabins. Many of the family would stay at the Big House rather than building a cabin.

When our family visited Guard for a weekend or a week, we sometimes stayed at the Big House, and sometimes at a cabin that wasn't being used at the time. My favorite cabin was the one called

"Overflow." It was right on Mill Run Creek, with its little dock, and the roaring creek was music to my ears. The creek no longer runs there. It was diverted many years ago by a giant storm. When visiting in 1992 I was disappointed to see the creek no longer there.

Each of the single cabins had a simple single electric line, due to the REA (Rural Electrification Association) efforts during the early 1930s. There was only enough electricity for ONE light bulb in each cabin. There were no phones, radios, or anything else electrical. Wood or coal fueled the stove. Toilet facilities were down the road at the outhouse behind the Big House. When mother decided we kids needed a bath, she would hand us each a towel and bar of soap, and we would go down to the creek to bathe. Very cold, glad I don't have to do that anymore! Each cabin had a sink, but no running water. Only a hand pump existed as the source of water; again we had to be careful to save a bucket of water to prime the pump. Each cabin had two bedrooms, one for parents, the other for kids.

The Driscoll sons and my father built the swimming pool about 1930 directly across the road from the Big House. It was about 30 by 30 feet, with one side shallow. A rope was across the pool at the edge of the shallow side so small kids would not enter the deep end, which was about eight feet deep. Water flow into and from the pool was conducted through a pipeline from the creek and another pipe at the other end of the pool back to the creek. The pipes, probably about two feet in diameter were covered with screens, to keep out undesirable animals. Sometimes the animals got in anyhow, perhaps by breaking the screens. Due to the drainage system, the pool would collect a lot of mud on the bottom, which necessitated draining the pool and shoveling out the mud on a regular basis. Nowadays, with the drainage system updated, that problem is apparently eliminated.

We would find an occasional mudpuppy (sometimes called waterdogs), often buried in the mud at the bottom of the pool. Ever see one of those things? Pretty ugly. We kids, all teenagers at the time, found one. One of the boys went to get his shotgun and shot the salamander three times, then we buried it. Three days later, just for kicks, we dug up the little monster, and it was still alive! You didn't want mud puppies in the pool. They can inflict terrible bites. Mudpuppies live in mud at the bottom of rivers or lakes. They have gills, like fish, and that enables them to live in the water.

There was a magnificent lawn beside the Big House, between it and the garden. All summer long Mom and Pop Driscoll would sit on the glider in the yard after dinner, when all the chores were done, and sometimes in the late afternoons before dinner. There were many pieces of lawn furniture and many huge pine trees, making this a beautiful shady retreat, even on the hottest days.

For as long as I can remember, Mom Driscoll had a maid helper named Lyda. She was a big Irish lady who lived with the family and helped wherever Mom Driscoll needed help. She helped mostly in the kitchen, especially at Guard. In the city (Connellsville) she saw to the laundry and other housekeeping chores. Lyda was a Godsend. She was a bit brusque, not familiar with people, but kind and extremely dutiful. Lyda seemed to be everywhere. She kept things running efficiently.

Pop Driscoll put in a huge vegetable garden adjacent to the Big House, big enough to feed the many members of his large and growing family. A white wood rail fence surrounded the huge garden. It must have been two or three acres in size. Every kind of vegetable was in that garden and rows and rows of corn. It seems that we had corn on the cob every time we ate there, all summer long. Many dinners consisted of corn-on-the-cob and fresh tomatoes and fresh homemade bread. These were the best meals. Pop Driscoll would often eat 20 ears of corn himself. He was a robust person!

Everyone in all the cabins and the Big House ate at the Big House for dinner every day. It was just the thing to do. The women staying in the various cabins would also come to help in the kitchen at dinner time. With so many to feed, lots of hands were needed.

Pop would go out into the garden where a giant bell hung from tall posts that were six or eight feet high. He would ring that bell to let everyone know that dinner would soon be served. You could hear that bell all up and down the valley. Even when we kids would be up on the mountain, we could hear it and knew it was time to come home. Up there on the mountain, we could even hear Pop sneeze, too, so loud and gusty were his sneezes and showed how sound carried through the valley.

We kids used to climb the mountain to near the top where giant pine trees grew. Many of the trees had huge long grapevines hanging to ground level. We would grab a grapevine, retreat further uphill, and then swing out over the valley. What sights we could see. People were little ants. It was thrilling! One day we all made our way up the mountain, as usual, to find every one of the grapevines gone. Doggone! Some adults ruined our fun!

After Mom and Pop Driscoll had died, and Lonesome Pine inherited by the oldest Driscoll son, they found termites riddled the Big House. It was torn down, and a simple three-bedroom, one-story house was constructed. There were no more huge dinners for 20 to 40 people at a time anymore.

As time went on, all the cabins were reconstructed, remodeled, and insulation, electricity and appliances added. The owners added indoor plumbing and bathrooms. The Post Office started mail delivery. Then the county paved the road. Guard is not the same place anymore. The magic is no longer there! The rustic, idyllic atmosphere is gone, replaced by a staid pedestrian neighborhood.

Mill Run Creek behind the “Overflow” cottage. We kids occasionally swam and played in this creek, along with other creatures like dragon flies, water striders and garter snakes. The water was crystal clear, so we could see quite well what we were swimming with.

The swimming pool at Guard that Dad and the Driscoll boys built about 1930. This was our summer fun place to be, especially when it was really hot. It had a deep end for diving and a shallow end for little kids.

Early Memories of Uncle Ike – the 1940s

It was Sunday, December 7, 1941. Mother and Dad were listening to opera on the radio in the living room, and dad reading the newspaper. I was playing in the corner of the living room. Suddenly, the announcer broke into the program and told the world that the Japanese had bombed Pearl Harbor.

Dad slowly lowered his newspaper and with a look of fright on his face as if he were seeing Armageddon, said "Oh – My – God" in slow, sonorous tones. (This was not a curse or an epithet, but a seeking help from God, a prayerful plea. In dangerous times, to whom do we turn? Regardless, it was the look on his face, and the terribleness of the tone of this voice as if he were seeing the end of the world. Besides which, he grew up in a very religious community – the River Brethren, a sect much like the Amish and Mennonites. The word "God" was NEVER to be used except in prayer.)

In my seven-year-old mind, I felt the world was coming to an end. The moment was frightening to me. Dad had never uttered such a dreadful proclamation! I can never forget that moment. And, he had never uttered the word "God" before for any reason.

In a few months, our lives would be turned upside down. Dwight, one of Dad's older brothers, would be named Commander-in-Chief of the Invasion Forces to head up the greatest army the world had ever seen. President Roosevelt declared war on Japan and then Germany. Dwight would be commissioned to head up the European forces to destroy Hitler.

One clarification – The Eisenhower brothers always called Dwight, "Dwight." However, to all his nieces and nephews, he always signed his letters "Uncle Ike." That's how we cousins knew him.

Uncle Ike kept up a regular correspondence with his many nieces and nephews, always remembering us on our birthdays and often at Christmas. In 1943, he sent Buddy an Italian officer's pistol (with the firing pin removed) and to me he sent the silken, braided red, white and blue rope used on his staff car. No, I didn't get the starred flag from his staff car, but it probably went to one of our cousins. Both of us got personally autographed pictures of him, and our cousins got similar pictures also autographed. The West Penn Newsletter featured a picture of Buddy and me with our new treasures. Buddy (he preferred to be called Earl, Jr. when he grew up) kept his pistol to the end of his life. I donated my flag rope to the Eisenhower Museum many years ago. The pictures we kept and have continued to occupy prominent spaces in our homes.

We were fortunate to have spent time with Uncle Ike. He would make it a point to visit all his brothers when he could. Just before he was sent to Washington to plan the D-Day Invasion, he visited all his brothers. He visited us in Lock 4. (North Charleroi was also known as "Lock 4" because of the lock and dam #4 on the Monongahela River. In fact you could mail a letter to "Earl Eisenhower, Lock 4, Pennsylvania and that was sufficient address to reach us.). Uncle Ike was a very "down-home" kind of person and never stood on protocol or demanded any special attention. He was always "just one of the boys."

As time and the war rolled on, he continued to write many letters to family, including nephews and nieces and far-flung cousins. I've always believed his letter writing held the brothers together, as far apart as they lived, for the duration of their lives. After the war, each and every summer they would plan a hunting or fishing trip to Northern

Wisconsin, Canada or other northern parts of the country. I remember one year when they hired a bush pilot to take them to a back woods area somewhere in Canada. The pilot dropped them off and came back a week later to pick them up. There was a small trading post in the area where they could get necessities.

July 17, 1946. Wisconsin fishing trip

In this place I would like to have had a picture showing my Father, Earl, vainly trying to extricate a fishhook from his pants, while the other brothers, Arthur, Milton, Dwight and Ed laugh uproariously. All the brothers signed the picture except Earl. Found in my papers some years ago, the original was turned over to the Eisenhower Library. This is my favorite photograph of the brothers, taken on a Wisconsin fishing trip in 1946.

However, the *Milwaukee Sentinel* never gave me permission to use the picture

Photo Earl Eisenhower Wisconsin July 1947

Permission from estate of Earl Eisenhower Sr.

One of my favorites, showing Uncle Ike with his famous potato salad. Whenever the brothers gathered, Ike was sure to be cooking. He was famous for his grilling for famous visitors – Churchill, cabinet members and others.

Fame descended upon us. It was relentless. Reporters showed up out of nowhere. We had very little privacy. Everything we did could be the subject of a newspaper article the next day. Fortunately, our friends who had known us for years were still our same old friends. They treated us the same as they always had. What we discovered, however, were "new-found" friends, eager for a piece of the spotlight. Mother hated the new found fame and the false friends. Dad took it in stride. I didn't give it much thought, until about 1949-1952, when I was in high school.

All of Uncle Ike's brothers experienced similar events. Unlike me, however, my cousins did not hit the spotlight as Buddy and I did, probably because of our ages. My cousins were all 12 years older and more, married, with children, and no thought or inclination of the fame that landed on our family.

Milton's children, Ruth and Bud, experienced some of the same, but perhaps not the same as I did. Ruth had a different experience: her mother, Helen Eakin Eisenhower, died in 1954 of breast cancer at the age of 49. Consequently, Ruth became her father's hostess when he entertained, which was a heavy responsibility for a 16-year-old.

Since Uncle Ike was constantly in the news, Mother stayed busy every evening clipping newspaper articles (we got both morning and evening newspapers each day) and pasted them into huge scrapbooks. Fifty years later the scrapbooks would be donated to the Eisenhower Library collections.

The War Years
Early 1940s

World War II hugely impacted our lives, in fact, everyone's lives. When a huge mobilization effort got underway after Roosevelt declared war on Japan and Germany, the nation's resources, being greatly under-utilized, had to be brought up to speed very quickly. Car production plants, for instance, were converted to making jeeps or tanks. Everyone had to pitch in.

Many women went to work in factories since the men were drafted.

Households saved tin foil (now we have aluminum foil), glass bottles, newspaper, and tin cans (cans were tin then). Teams of men collected that stuff, tossing it into special trucks that were just open-flat-bed trucks with solid sides. Garbage men would collect each homeowner's can of garbage by jumping off the back of the truck as it slowed for each stop. They would then pick up a garbage can and heave its contents over their head into the dump truck. Later on garbage trucks were constructed with compacters and the men didn't have to heave the cans of garbage so high. Garbage cans had to be thoroughly cleaned each week after being emptied. We had no plastic bags then for garbage, nor did we have garbage disposers. We rolled daily garbage in newspapers, depositing each day's bundle in the large cans to be collected weekly. You can imagine what the smell was like at the end of the week.

Rationing became the law. Everything was rationed. There were coupons for shoes, galoshes, nylons, gasoline, canned goods, coffee, cheese, canned milk, sugar, salt, meat, and other stuff. Bath tissue such as Kleenex was no longer manufactured. Toilet paper was still manufactured, though, but it may have also been rationed.

After the war, when Kleenex was again on store shelves, I was so excited to see Kleenex again, that I took several sheets and lined my doll's bunk beds. Mother was appalled when she discovered what I had done with the precious tissue.

Each home had a ration book with pages of coupons – coupons for meat, sugar, shoes, etc., depending on the size of your family. The coupon books were delivered monthly to each family. If more than one needed shoes, you might have to wait until next month for a shoes coupon. Some women would get together and trade coupons, depending on what each might need for their family.

The government devised the rationing system in order to prevent black marketing of scarce items and food.

Our family had no gasoline rationing because Dad was chief engineer for the power company, and if there were emergencies, he would have to answer the call. He had a mid-30s black Ford Coupe as a company car, and we had our 1941 Blue Humpback Ford and unlimited gasoline for both. Vehicles that had unrestricted gasoline purchases had special stickers.

We were very fortunate that Dad had a small acreage in the country owned by our landlord, Mr. Wise, who allowed dad to farm it. Dad was a farmer all his life. He grew almost every kind of vegetable known to man that would grow in Pennsylvania. When he was growing up in Kansas, their small farm was their existence and livelihood. Each of the six boys had a plot to farm and had the choice of what to grow. He and Milton, the two youngest, would work together, growing, harvesting and selling the excess after family needs were met. Each boy learned how to manage his income, and preserve food either by canning or in the root cellar.

At the end of every summer, our kitchen became the center of food preservation. Mother was at the stove canning, we kids sat at the large kitchen table popping peas, shucking corn, snapping beans, or helping with other vegetables. Dad managed the boiler in the cellar where the jars of vegetables or tomatoes were cooked for a length of time; they also used a pressure cooker. Canning was a lot of work, lasting for days on end when the weather was very hot. No one had ever heard of air conditioning, either. The kitchen was a sweatshop.

Another preservation method was that used for root vegetables. Dad would dig up all the potatoes at the end of the season before winter, dig a huge hole in the ground, put all the potatoes in it and cover it up with loose dirt. Anytime we needed potatoes, dad would go to his small plot of farmland and dig up some potatoes. We did not have store-bought vegetables.

Almost every day after work in the summer, Dad would come home, change into his farming clothes and gather up his farming tools. He then called Buddy and me (we were his slave helpers), and we headed to the country and his garden plot. As we got older, we were allowed to take our new bikes. After we had completed our garden chores, we were allowed to ride our new bikes along the old Coyle-Curtain country road. Now, it is so built-up we don't recognize it, but at that time it was all farmland, bucolic scenery with cows and other farm animals grazing peacefully everywhere.

At the end of each gardening day when vegetables were being harvested, Buddy and I got to take our little baskets of vegetables around the neighborhood and sell them. People were eager to buy our vegetables since coupons limited what people could buy in the stores. Good, fresh food was hard to come by, and most people did not have farming privileges. What money we made was ours to keep. Even after the war when rationing was over, people were still glad to buy our vegetables. Fresh from the garden always beats store bought.

Because we had a family car and unlimited gasoline, and our neighbors did not, Dad would take us kids on outings on summer Sundays. All the neighbor kids would gather around, and Dad would tell them, "Go ask your parents if you can go for a ride with us." All the kids would dash home and come running back, eager for a ride to wherever Mr. Eisenhower would take them. We would have six, seven and even eight kids stashed in our 1941 Ford. What fun that was! Usually, we would go up into the hills near

Uniontown or to Ohiopyle or other scenic such places. Usually, the place he took us would be near a creek. Sometimes we would go as far as Guard, which was about an hour or so away. Nevertheless, those trips on Sunday afternoons bring back wonderful memories.

THE PIANO

When I was ten years old, my begging for a piano finally got to my parents. They broke down and bought an old upright, which they tucked into the corner of the living room, next to the fireplace. Then, they contacted a local music teacher and arranged for her to teach me.

I took to the piano like a duck to water. After a couple of years, my teacher informed my parents that she could teach me no more. She claimed I knew as much if not more than she did. She recommended Dr. Veon, a professor of music at California State Teachers College (just upriver near Belle Vernon). He usually taught only the graduate students, but would take other prodigies upon passing his audition requirements.

My parents contacted him, and he agreed to audition me. His studio in Charleroi was a small walkup room in the middle of town. I went there one day to follow his instructions as to what was required of his pupils: for the audition, Claire de

Lune, and the second selection I don't remember. His philosophy was that anyone who could play Claire de Lune correctly was worthy of his teaching skills. After hearing me play, he agreed to accept me as a pupil.

One of his requirements at each weekly lesson was to play the scales and certain exercises. He also insisted on the pupil singing the scales along with playing them.

After the first scale performance from me, he was holding his ears and exclaiming, "Stop! Stop! I don't want to hear you sing anymore!" Then he went on to say, "I can't understand how someone who can play as well as you cannot sing!" I was twelve years old, and nothing has changed. I still can't sing.

I never could carry a tune in a bucket. His reaction to my singing voice I thought was really funny. He was the archetypal college professor – wispy white hair, always seeming to need combing, scruffy suits that he apparently cared little for and the stained tie. Since Kleenex was not manufactured until after the war, his pockets always had ribbons of toilet paper dangling from them. He was extremely strict and would not countenance any lateness in arrival or sloppiness in performance. Lessons were to be practiced and learned. If you did not practice, and learn, he would terminate his teaching of you.

I went on to be a concert pianist around the valley – giving mini-concerts in different areas, for clubs, church groups, etc. My repertoire was huge, as I had (catch that word – "had") a photographic memory. After I had practiced a piece of music a few times, the music was embedded in my brain. I did not need sheet music. I could close my eyes and see the music in my mind.

For various audiences, I usually would choose something from Tchaikovsky and other composers as well. The audiences would give me a standing ovation. That proves that people do appreciate classical music well presented. There were times when I was deep in the throes of playing some composition that I would feel like "something else" had taken command of my body and was playing, not me. It was an eerie feeling. When I got standing ovations, I "knew" that I was not the one playing!!!

In my last years of high school, I gave up the concert routine. Everyone I knew expected I would go to Juilliard. I was not interested. New York City was anathema to me, and I had no desire to go there. Then, at that time, I discovered people. Real people. Up to that time, I had to spend six to eight hours a day practicing the piano and rehearsing my total repertoire. For the first time in my life, I got to know people. Being attached to the piano several hours a day didn't allow me that privilege.

For years, I continued to play the piano, accompanying people and choral groups in high school, playing in church, playing for 4-H groups and other groups. I thoroughly enjoyed such piano playing. I put my piano playing skills to good use over the years.

Abilene Homecoming - 1945
My Second Major Trip

During the whole course of the war, in spite of Uncle Ike's tremendous responsibilities, correspondence between the Eisenhower brothers was voluminous. Many of the letters received from Uncle Ike were heavily redacted. I always thought it strange that the top General of the Army would be subject to such heavy-handed censorship. The brothers would write letters back and forth to each other, with carbon copies to all the brothers at the same time. If a letter were to Arthur, for instance, carbon copies would be sent to Ed, Dwight, my Dad, and Milton. We don't have "carbon copies" anymore – that is ancient! All the letters were hand-written, except Uncle Ike's. He had a secretarial staff!

Planning instigated by Uncle Ike assured the family of a reunion when the war was over. Uncle Ike was foremost in family communications and traditions. It is amazing how many letters he wrote. He never forgot a birthday of any of his relatives – nieces, nephews, cousins, brothers and close friends, and especially his mother. His father had died in 1942, and Uncle Ike was not able to go home for his funeral. He was in the War Department planning the invasion. How he kept up the letter writing, even while President, boggles my mind. He did, however, have very efficient secretaries upon whom he relied.

In June 1945, the war in Europe was over, and the Allies had conquered the Germans and Italians. The war in the Pacific would go on for a couple more months until August when Japan surrendered after the U.S. dropped atomic bombs on Hiroshima and Nagasaki.

Uncle Ike's first order of business was greeting his mother Ida, Mamie, Johnny, and all his far-flung brothers and their families in Abilene. The Eisenhower family has a ton of relatives, many who still reside in Kansas. The reunion included all of these many relatives.

Uncle Ike no sooner landed on these shores again, than a ticker-tape parade in New York City was held in his honor. A ticker-tape parade is an amazing thing to see. I wasn't there in person but saw lots of pictures. Uncle Ike was smiling and waving throughout the whole ordeal, but secretly he wanted just to be with Mamie and his family.

He had been many long years away from Mamie and son Johnny, with very few interludes to join them during the course of the war.

The plan, as envisioned by Uncle Ike, was for all the brothers and their families to meet in Kansas City. From there, we all would take a special train to Abilene where Ida and other family members would be waiting to greet us.

The first leg of our family's journey, leaving North Charleroi, took us to Pittsburgh, where we took a train to Chicago.

Sun-Telegraph Photo.

LEAVING TO JOIN 'IKE'— En route to see his brother, Gen. Dwight Eisenhower, Earl D. Eisenhower prepares to board a westbound train at Pennsylvania Station with wife and children. They're from North Charleroi.

Newspaper picture, probably Pittsburgh Press

Picture taken while our family was getting ready to board a train to Chicago, an interim stop on our way to Abilene. Pictured, left to right: Earl Sr., Kaye, Buddy (Earl Jr.) and Kathryn (Earl's wife)

Planning this trip was not so simple as it sounds. Soldiers were returning from Europe by the tens of thousands. There was no such thing as plane travel at this time – well, not for the ordinary person. Plane travel was just getting initiated, and the plane travelers were few and far between.

Railroads were putting on extra trains and extra cars on each train to accommodate the hordes of soldiers making their way from the east coast to the heartland where their homes were. Everywhere we looked was pandemonium. It was chaos! When we got to Union Station in Pittsburgh, the railroad had added so many extra trains and cars we didn't know where to go. Fortunately, a Porter who took charge of our luggage had the good sense to know which train on which to put our baggage. The crowds in the railway station were so dense you could hardly turn around. We didn't know which train to get on due to the confusion of all the extra trains. Fearing that we had lost all our luggage, we got on the train the Porter directed us. We were on the train but had no idea where our luggage was. Dad tipped a Porter and told him to see what he could do. Eventually, later that night, the Porter showed up with our luggage. Another porter had, fortunately, put our luggage on the right train.

The train trip to Chicago was about a day. It was literally so packed with soldiers it was standing room only. Our family had sleeping compartments, fortunately.

The extreme number of people (mostly soldiers) constantly filled the dining car. Mother, Dad, Buddy and I, got in line for the dining car and waited with the others. The line for the dining car was two or three cars long. Suddenly, we were being pushed forward, past the lines of soldiers waiting their turn. These soldiers had learned that dad was Dwight Eisenhower's brother, and they felt that any relative of Dwight Eisenhower was deserving of royal treatment. As we were pushed forward to the dining car ahead of all those soldiers waiting in line, they cheered us! The adoration and respect for my uncle were unbelievable! They gave up their spot in line for Dwight Eisenhower's brother! The reverence they had for their General was awesome to behold. These soldiers probably wondered how or why a "civilian" was aboard this train! They found out!

We changed trains in Chicago for another that took us to Kansas City. We still received the royal treatment. How did all these soldiers learn that we were Eisenhowers?

Arriving in Kansas City, all the brothers met at the Muehlebach Hotel, where we stayed one night. (History of this historic hotel can be found online at Wikipedia.com and other sites.) From there the plan was to board a special train to Abilene. If I remember rightly, trains to Abilene were few and far between, so to arrange this train required special preparations.

When our special train arrived in Abilene, with all my uncles, their wives, and families, Grandmother Ida was waiting at the station, along with other family and her caregiver. Grandma was becoming a bit "dotty" as we would say. She knew people and could converse quite well, could do things for herself, but couldn't remember the time of day. She was 85 years old and would pass on within the year.

All of us Eisenhower families stayed at the Sunflower Hotel during our stay in Abilene. It is now on the National Register of Historic Places. Built in 1931 by a consortium of noted Abilene executives, it was one of only two hotels in this country at the time that had air conditioning. It also was the only hotel between Denver and Kansas City that a telephone and radio in each room. The Sunflower Hotel became known as "The Little White House," for the frequent trips President Eisenhower would make there in later years. The east end of the sixth floor became the "Presidential Suite," always refurbished prior to each visit the future President would make. The history of this historic hotel is available online at http://www.kshs.org/resource/national_register/nominationsNRDB/Dickinson_HotelSunflowerNR.pdf

Grandma Ida was so excited to see her sons – all of them together, which had not happened since 1926 when all her sons came home at the same time to celebrate a family reunion. Usually, one son or another would visit each year.

The festivities began.

One event I remember quite well is sitting on the front porch with grandma and other family members, when a group of newspapermen and photographers approached us.

One of the journalists asked grandma, "Aren't you proud of your son?"

Ida replied, "Which one?"

I was sitting next to her when this occurred, though I am not in the picture, which was published throughout the nation with this famous quote: "Which One?" Nobody could believe that she would say such a thing, but knowing Grandma Ida, I fully understand her reply.

Ida was right. She was indeed proud of every single one of her sons. Each had achieved the highest in his chosen profession. For a poor farm family from Abilene, Kansas, this was a remarkable thing. Boys in that day and age quit school after eighth grade to work on family farms. But, all six of the Eisenhower boys graduated from high school and five of the six went on to college. Wondering how this could be so caused me to research and write my first book, The Eisenhower Legacy

June 1945 – Five Eisenhower brothers with mother Ida.

Description of picture:

Grandma Ida is sitting in her rocking chair on the front porch of her home. Sitting on the top porch step at her feet, looking up at her, is Uncle Ike in his tan shirt and pants. Standing behind Grandma Ida are Arthur, Earl, Milton, and Ed

I was sitting on the porch next to them, across from Uncle Ike, when this photo was taken. This was the occasion when Grandma was asked if she was proud of her son, and she replied "Which one?"

This picture is from a collection of Myron Davis when he was freelancing for Life Magazine. Life never replied to my inquiries asking for permission to print this picture.

The Festivities and celebrations continued in Abilene for about a week, leaving time for all our relatives from all over Kansas to have a chance to greet Uncle Ike and have their picture taken with him. I remember one long day (for him) when person after person waited to have their picture taken with him. There were numerous cousins living in Kansas plus many old high school buddies. By the end of the day, Uncle Ike was looking tired and bored. Wouldn't you be also?

Buddy and I with Uncle Ike, June 1945, Abilene

Buddy and I with Uncle Ike. Uncle Ike is standing between Buddy and me, with his arms around us. Buddy is on his right and I on his left. This was the occasion when many people were lining up to have their picture taken with Uncle Ike. I believe the photo sessions went on all day. This picture was stamped with Myron Davis' stamp when he was taking pictures for Life Magazine. Life never replied to my query to print the picture.

Another special event I remember well is when photographers from all the newspapers wanted a special picture of Dwight with all his family on the special train that brought us to Abilene. (I believe this is the same car that Uncle Ike used in his campaign in 1952.) I got to go along, as did Buddy. Not all the family wished to go – my Dad is not there, neither is Mamie, nor my mother. Johnny was with us. I believe he is the one on the far left, partially hidden by Aunt Helen, but it is hard to make him out in this picture.

Abilene Reflector-Chronicle – permission granted by the Reflector Chronicle

Pictured are Helen Eaken Eisenhower (wife of Milton), Katherine Eisenhower Roeuche'(daughter of Arthur), Louise Eisenhower (wife of Arthur), Kaye Eisenhower (daughter of Earl), Edgar

Eisenhower, Buddy Eisenhower (Earl, Jr.), Arthur, Ike, Milton Eisenhower. Johnny is hidden behind Aunt Helen on the far left. Taken on the caboose of the train that brought us to Abilene. Uncle Ike later used this train in his barnstorming tour when running for President.

We younger cousins – Buddy (9) and I (11), my cousin Ruth (7) and her brother Bud (15), were provided two Jeeps so we could ride around Abilene. The drivers were specially assigned military personnel. All our other cousins were 12 years older and more, married with children, and had no interest in riding around in Jeeps. We had two Jeeps, each with Walkie-Talkies. Walkie-talkies were the forerunner of CB radios. We had such fun riding all over Abilene, talking back and forth with our Walkie-Talkies. We must have made quite a bit of noise as we rode up and down the streets of Abilene. There were thousands of people in town for festivities and to greet Ike, many of them his old friends and cousins from childhood days.

Banners and bunting festooned the whole town and thousands of people from all over Kansas, and the Midwest had shown up to greet Ike, including friends, family, cousins from everywhere.

When our families first gathered at the Sunflower Hotel, all gathered in one room, and the fun began. It was quite a squish. The Eisenhower brothers' favorite sport was arguing, just for fun, to see who could get the best of the rest. One, for instance, would say black was black, and another would say black was white, and the game was on! The women and children would sit around the perimeter of the room and listen. It was a sideshow. I loved it. Women and children were not allowed to participate. We were the "peanut gallery," as my brother used to say.

The first order of business, however, was to find some booze. Abilene was a dry town, as was the whole state of Kansas. Recognizing this need, Uncle Ed grabbed the largest suitcase he could find, emptied all the contents on the middle of the bed, closed it up and left the room with the suitcase. He returned about a half hour later, deposited the suitcase on the bed and opened it, to reveal a full load of any whiskey one might want.

Dad asked, "Ed, where did you get all that stuff?"

Ed replied, "I'll never tell!"

The Eisenhower brothers were always a raucous bunch, laughing, shouting, talking over each other. Women and children in the room would be relegated to the fringes, the perimeter, not to take part in the repartee, but to be onlookers.

Life was a multi-part play, and they were the actors on stage. They argued with each other, getting louder as time went on. Their favorite sport was to argue with each other, always in good fun. I don't remember all the subjects discussed, but their rambunctious repartee bounced from subject to subject.

The six boys grew up in a very close-knit family, each with their personality, responsibilities, talents, friendships, likes and dislikes. However, their differences belied what their closeness was. If one was attacked, the brothers would gather around to protect and defend the dishonored one.

Abilene Reflector-Chronicle – permission granted by the Reflector-Chronicle

Eisenhower reunion at the Sunflower Hotel in Abilene 1945:

(seated) Louise Grieb Eisenhower (Arthur's wife), Lloyd Edgar Eisenhower (Roy's son, "Bud"), Arthur Bradford Roueche' (Arthur's grandson), Milton Stover Eisenhower Jr. ("Bud"), Earl Dewey Eisenhower Jr. ("Buddy"), John Sheldon Doud Eisenhower, Mamie Doud Eisenhower, Mrs. Paul Lucas, Paul Lucas (cousin of the Eisenhower brothers), Ruth Eakin Eisenhower (daughter of Milton Sr.), Milton Stover Eisenhower Sr.

(standing) Katherine Eisenhower Roeuche'(Arthur's daughter), Arthur Bradford Eisenhower, Kathryn (Kaye) Snyder Eisenhower, Kathryn Snyder Eisenhower (wife of Earl Sr.), Earl Dewey Eisenhower Sr., Edgar Newton Eisenhower, Bernice Eisenhower (Edgar's second wife), Patricia Eisenhower (daughter of Roy Eisenhower), Peggy Jane Eisenhower (daughter of Roy), Helen Eakin Eisenhower (wife of Milton Sr.), Edna Shade Eisenhower (Roy's widow).

The trip home was anti-climatic, to say the least.

Fun Stuff and Chores
1940s

We didn't have fancy toys, computers, TVs and other forms of entertainment. We had to make our fun. People had radios, but that was all. They were stationary, plugged into an electrical outlet, not the kind you could carry around. Each home had one radio and one telephone. In our area, the phone was a rotary dial one. Our phone number was 467. The local movie theater number was 476.

Often mother would answer the phone, and someone would ask, "What's playing today?"

Mother would answer, "My kids," and hang up the phone.

Everyone else had party lines. We had a private line because of dad's job, having to be on call for power emergencies, so the power company paid the difference for a private line.

To call someone, we would pick up the receiver and dial the operator, and then tell the operator the number you wanted or the name of the person you wanted. If we knew our friend's number, we could dial it on the rotary dial on the front of the phone. There was a central switchboard somewhere in town. If you had a party line, often a neighbor would be talking on the phone, and you would have to wait until they hung up before using the phone. If you had a party line, one ring would be for one family, two rings for another family, three rings for another, etc.

Our friends living out in the country had phones that were big wooden boxes on the wall. In order to make a call, they had to rotate the lever to contact the operator who would then come on and make calls for them.

When we kids were growing up, we were allowed a maximum of five minutes on the phone. Period. It was important to keep the line clear for dad's business. Some people had party lines; consequently, others could pick up their phone and listen in on your conversation. If you had to make a phone call, you might have to wait until the other people were off the phone.

Besides washing and drying dishes every evening after dinner, Buddy and I had our regular chores every Saturday. Mother diligently oversaw our chores: one of us had to scrub and wax the linoleum kitchen floor; the other had to scrub the entire bathroom. Buddy and I took turns with these tasks each Saturday. There were other regular chores, too, like helping mother to polish the furniture, carry out the garbage and take the ashes out of the furnace. We had a coal furnace in the basement, and each week the ashes that fell through the grate to the bottom had to be shoveled out. That was Buddy's chore; I never had to shovel ashes.

Coal deliveries came through our basement window (or trap door) in the front of the house at ground level. The coal truck would back up to the front of the house, lower the chute, raise the bed of the truck and the coal would slide into the coal cellar. Dad always bought a grade of coal called "pea" coal, which apparently burned cleaner than regular coal. The coal cellar was closed off from the rest of the cellar, and the door opened only once a day to put more coal in the furnace. The hot air from the furnace rose through giant ducts to all rooms in the house. Consequently, everything became coated eventually with coal dust, which is why we had two "spring cleanings" per year instead of one. Mother and Dad would get huge chunks of wallpaper cleaner, which became the Play-Doh of later years. The wallpaper cleaning would begin. It would take all day.

Sometimes we kids would get a lump of coal and grow crystals by putting it in a dish of water and adding baking soda or other stuff.

We had fertile imaginations when it came to playing since we had to invent our own. One time, around Halloween, Buddy and I decided to put together a dummy. We found a mask, old overalls, shirt, shoes and hat that we stuffed with straw. After putting this together, we hung it from a Maple tree branch that overhung the main highway (Route 88). The tree was cut down many years ago. It was right over a streetlight where the dummy was easily seen. We waited on the front porch, which was closed in by a solid brick railing topped with cement slab. As cars came roaring down the highway, topping the small rise at the entrance to our street (Pennsylvania Avenue), seeing the "body" hanging from the tree, drivers would slam on the brakes. Buddy and I were hiding behind the brick wall of the porch rolling around with laughter. We thought the screeching cars, repeated over and over, was so funny. Mother and Dad, in the living room, became curious as to why all the screeching of brakes and stepped out onto the porch to investigate. There they found Buddy and me, laughing hilariously. Dad ordered us to take down the dummy. Well, we did that, but then decided to lay the dummy in the middle of the road. We did take down the dummy. The screeching brakes continued. When dad had to come out a second time, he ordered us to bed. Oh, well, we had fun while it lasted.

Another of our favorite pastimes was to count cars. We kids, any number, would gather on our front porch, which was right on the main highway (Route 88) from Pittsburgh. There would be lots of cars at times. We each would choose which car we would count: Chevy, Ford, Dodge, or "truck." As each car or truck went by we would keep count. At the end of our counting period, however, long it might be, the winner, of course, was the one who had the highest count. Chevy or Ford usually won.

We also used to play baseball in the alley beside our house. At the first crack of the bat, I was out there with the boys, playing with them. We did use a baseball, too. Baseball was much more fun than dolls. I "caught" a line drive as I was playing first base one time. It was no great feat. It came straight at me and caught me in the stomach! Oooof! That took the wind out of me. Then the cheers for catching the ball were, I felt, rather misplaced because I didn't catch the ball – it caught me, so to speak!

When I was little, I was quite jealous of boys. They had all the fun! Cars, trucks, trains, tinker toys, erector sets, etc. We girls always got dolls and coloring books. When I woke up in the morning, I would quickly get dressed, grab my brother's toy trucks and cars and head for the driveway behind our house, which was dirt covered with red dog. Red dog was the gravel-like substance remaining after processing the iron ore. Dad would put a cover in the trunk of the car, drive over to the mill/smelter and gather a huge load of "red dog." The red dog was used to cover the driveway, as we use gravel now, to cover the dirt, which otherwise would be a sea of mud when it rained. I would shovel aside an area of red dog and create little roads through the dirt for all the little cars. To this day, I love digging in the dirt, planting stuff.

When I was very young, about six, we were at a West Penn Picnic, a yearly event usually held at a large park, like Kennywood Park. I had never been on a slide before and seeing all the kids go down this marvelous contraption, I wanted to go too. Well, I did, but I didn't know how to land on my feet. I hit the ground on my rear end and oh, the pain was unbearable. I was screaming in pain. Dad and his friend John Rhea came to my rescue, each taking one of my arms and guiding me back to the picnic benches. I was in so much pain, but no one paid any attention to me.

Dad just said, "Oh, you'll be OK in a little while."

Right! Many years later, almost nine months pregnant with my first child, the custom with doctors then was to X-ray the abdomen of the mother-to-be to see if the fetus was in the correct position. The doctor discovered that I had a fractured tailbone. That's why I endured so much pain for so many years. It took years for that tailbone to heal. So much for "Oh, it will be OK." I endured so much pain for so many years, I learned to keep my mouth shut. Who would believe me? And, who wanted to know? To this day, I do not complain of pain. It comes with aging, like it or not.

We would get a good whipping for the least infraction of rules. If I weren't sure what the rules might be, I'd talk Buddy into doing something. If he were punished, I figured I didn't want to do that.

Kids in the neighborhood often made stink bombs. That was not a nice thing to do. I did it once, but never again. The trick was to put the ingredients in a paper sack, put it in front of a door and ring the doorbell. We would run like the wind and hide, waiting for the homeowner to open the door to find the stench!. And it was awful!

Most of the time we kids – about eight to twelve of us in the neighborhood – played games on Sheppard Avenue. We played Mother May I, Hopscotch, Simon Says, touch football, baseball, marbles, and Hide & Seek. In bad weather we played jacks or pick-up-sticks inside, or board games such as Monopoly, Parcheesi, or checkers. When I was a teenager I played chess with Andy, son of another West Penner, who lived in our neighborhood. (Andy and I were buddies – he and I were more like brother and sister. I went with him to a W&J weekend party when Andy's regular girlfriend couldn't make it. We had great fun because we were the only couple not necking.)

Neighborhoods were safe. We kids could play outside all day long and needn't come home until Mother called us at dinnertime. We knew our boundaries. In the summer we did not have to come inside until the streetlights came on, which was generally about 9 to 10 PM. Mother didn't have to call us; we knew we had to be home, or else!

Summer evenings would find us chasing lightning bugs – or fireflies. We would run in the house, grab a mason jar, and then see who could catch the most lightning bugs. When we went to bed, we let all the lightning bugs go. Otherwise, they would be dead in the morning.

In the summer, when it was hot, the firemen would come to our neighborhood and turn on the sprinkler. It was a pipe, connected to the fire hydrant, with holes in it about eight feet above the street, stretching across the street. All us kids would run home and put on our bathing suits and run back and forth under the sprinkler. That was fun on hot summer days.

We had roller skates – these were metal platforms with four metal wheels that we attached to the soles of our shoes with clamps. And we had scooters – big enough for two, metal, with big rubber wheels and the red wagon – Radio Flyer. Eventually Buddy and I had our Schwinn bikes. We no longer had to share with friends. The bikes were a surprise Christmas gift from Dad's friend, Dr. Sickman, at Christmas 1944; probably the first year non-military stuff was on the market. I was ten, Buddy eight. We were beside ourselves with joy at having our bikes. Now, we could go riding miles out in the country with other kids and not have to stay forlornly behind when the others headed out on their bike rides. What joy! Out Route 88 and up the steep hill to the Coyle residence, where we turned left and went out the old Coyle-Curtain Road to the top of the hill in Lock 4 where the water tower was. This route at the time was all rural farmland. From there it was a very steep straight downhill ride home to Pennsylvania Avenue.

In the winter, we had lots of places to sled ride. Hills were everywhere. The alley beside our house was perfect. When there was plenty of snow, which was often, we built a huge hump across the alley like a ski jump. Starting at the top of the alley by the main highway, we pushed hard for a flying start and went flying off the hump and down the hill. We could do that all day. What fun! We didn't have real skis but made our own from old curtain rods. That sufficed, but they weren't too effective. Real skis would have been better, but who could afford such things?

During the War, the local Coyle Movie Theater would get newsreels. Almost every newsreel featured Uncle Ike or the soldiers or the war. Then, Mr. Coyle would call Dad or Mother and arrange for us to go to the theater just to view the newsreel. Buddy and I would usually beg Dad to let us stay and watch the cartoons that followed the newsreel. Sometimes we could, but most often, not.

No one had television in those days. We got our news from newspapers, radio, or newsreels at the movie theater. I think the first television set showed up in our neighborhood around 1950. Dad refused to buy a TV until after we moved to Chicago in 1954. They were small and clunky and came in a cabinet. The picture (black and white) was probably about ten inches wide. The only shows were The Ed Sullivan Show, and boxing.

Fishing was a great sport, Dad's favorite. He taught Buddy and me how to cast and bought us our very own fly rods and reels. We often went to the country to a lake or stream. I got very good at casting though I don't remember ever catching a fish. I remember seeing two little boys one day, sitting on a bridge over a stream, with nothing more than a stick and bent pins for hooks. They were catching fish by the barrelful, and I hadn't caught anything with my fancy rod and reel. So much for fancy!

Dad was a character. He was very strict with us kids. But when he was out with his poker-playing friends drinking beer at the Turners Club (the German Turn Verein club), or with friends, he could be funny and good natured.

The people Dad worked with remembered him as "quite a guy." A lady I met recently, who worked with him in the office, commented on their lunchtime rituals. People gathered around, and Dad told stories of his travels and childhood, keeping everyone enthralled and sometimes in stitches. One man remarked, "He was very genuine, someone I thoroughly enjoyed." Uncle Ike once called his brother at work during the lunch period. He remarked to one of his co-workers that Dwight had called to make sure "I had a decent suit for the inauguration." Dad would hand out "I

Like Ike" buttons to people at work. They kept them and passed them on to family members.

Dad also taught electrical engineering at a college in Uniontown for the evening classes. When we got a lot of snow, which was often, he would be quite late getting home, as roads were almost impassable, and he would have to stop and put chains on the tires. The roads in Pennsylvania were narrow, twisting, high-crowned roads, making it difficult to maneuver at times, especially when there was a lot of snow.

One of our rituals was gym class every Saturday morning at the German Turn Verein (or Turners Club). The gymnasium was upstairs, over the bar and ballroom. Dad would play poker with his friends in the barroom while Buddy and I attended our gym classes. That's the German upbringing from Dad's perspective – feed the mind, the body, and the soul in order to be a harmonious person. The Turners Club was designed originally like a speakeasy, converted to a private club after Prohibition ended. We had to knock at the door, someone would come and look through the little window, and if you were a recognized member, the door would be opened for you.

Dad and Mom had a large group of friends with whom they partied, played bridge or whatever.

Booze usually flowed freely. One of their friends mentioned to Dad one time that he cussed a lot.

Dad said, "Oh, no I don't!"

To prove a point, one of the guys placed a tape recorder under the sofa where Dad was sitting one evening when a lot of people were partying. At the end of the evening, the tape was re-played.

Dad was thunderstruck. He never realized that he had been swearing so much. Seems like swear words were sprinkled liberally throughout his conversation that evening. From then on, he made a huge effort to clean up his habit. I never heard him swear when I was growing up. He was apparently aware of the effect on us kids.

In 1944, when I was ten and Buddy eight, Dad took us out to the country to a dog breeder's farm. There, we had a chance to pick out our very own dog – a toy Manchester Terrier. We picked a little one who was a real live wire, and named her Ginger. Mother was aghast! She hated dogs, and knew she would be stuck at home every day with the dog since we kids were in school and Dad at work. Buddy and I did have to walk her twice a day, and make sure she was fed and bathed regularly. Dad always felt that having a dog was a good thing for children. When he was young, he and his brothers found a stray dog, which apparently had come from a circus. He was a little terrier and from that time on, terriers were the only dogs worth considering as far as Dad was concerned. Ginger was a pistol! One time she got ahold of a pillow in my brother's room (the sleeping porch) and had the pillow totally shredded and feathers from one end of the room to the other. Mother was furious! Another time when the meter reader came to read our electric meter (meters were in the basements at that time), Ginger got loose, jumped at him and bit him in the rear. Fortunately, since it was the Electric company meter man, the West Penn did not sue us. Our front porch entry door to the living room had a long window, which was covered with a curtain. Every time someone walked by the house, Ginger would take a flying leap at the door, hitting the curtain. It didn't take long for the curtain to become shredded. We would take Ginger for walks in the neighborhood. Dr. Miksch, our neighbor, had a purebred Doberman, which his daughter used to walk every day. Ginger, looking like a tiny Doberman, would race in circles around the Doberman and that dog would stand and watch our crazy dog, as if to say "What in the world is that thing?" In 1954 we had to give up Ginger. We were moving to a rented home in La Grange which did not allow dogs. I cried for two weeks. Mother was overjoyed!

One time Dad was driving home fairly late in the evening, and a cop stopped him for speeding. When asked for his driver's license, Dad handed it over. The cop looked at it, handed it back, and said, "Have a nice evening, Mr. Eisenhower." So much for being an Eisenhower. The perks aren't bad at times.

Another time in 1956 when Dad and Mom were planning on attending the Republican Convention in San Francisco, we were living in La Grange, near Chicago, where the CB&Q Railroad passed through. The express train (The San Francisco Express) that ran straight through from Chicago to San Francisco did NOT stop anywhere until it got to its destination, San Francisco. There were similar express trains to Los Angeles and Denver. Living just a few miles from Union Station, Dad figured, "why not?" He called the head of the CB&Q Railroad and requested that the train stop to pick him and Mother up in La Grange. This was unheard of. The express train had never stopped here before. But, they did so at Dad's request. See, at times it pays to be an Eisenhower. The name was magic!

Starting when we were age six or school age, Dad insisted we go to Sunday School every Sunday – there was NO time off. I would try to hide under the covers and beg for one day to sleep in and dad's stentorian voice commanded, "Get up, you are going to church!" Well, I couldn't argue with that.

After a couple years of Sunday School, at about age eight, I discovered church and our Scottish preacher. I loved that man. He had a unique way of getting children's attention, and consequently the adults also. At the start of the sermon, he did a children's sermon that was the object of the adult sermon that day. Apparently the adults liked it too.

After I had discovered church, I called home one day and asked if I could stay for church, too. Dad used to take us to Sunday School, and then pick us up before church started, bringing old Mrs. Wigham, our next door neighbor, to church as no one in her family had a car.

This Methodist church I attended until I graduated from high school. I was an active member of the Youth Group. Year after year, the Methodists tried to get me to join the church, and Mother and Dad would not let me do it. At the time, the Methodists did not drink, smoke, play cards or dance. My parents insisted that I had no idea where I would be in the years ahead, and to make a vow and break it is a bad thing. In the following years, I did my share of drinking, smoking, card playing, and dancing, so I would not have made a good Methodist.

Our church youth group was the highlight of my social life. We had a large group of kids, with Mr. and Mrs. Frees as our chaperones and leaders.

Our church youth group went on a picnic one Sunday afternoon at an area in the Youghiogheny (commonly called the "Yock") wilderness area. Being too adventuresome, four of us decided to hike down to the Youghiogheny River, which we could see from the top of the hill. It was a very dense wilderness and quite steep. We kept losing the winding path and would go straight downhill to the next path we found, eventually getting to the bottom of the hill. We stayed for a while, enjoying the sight of this beautiful whitewater river. When it was time to start back up the hill, we lost the path. We figured that we could go straight up the hill till we found the path again but got hopelessly lost. It was beginning to get dark.

People missed us and called the State Police, who called our parents to tell them they were searching for us. We were lucky they found us. We were very scared. When the State Police found us, they were angry with us. They told us what idiots we were and that searchers never found lost people here, and that there were bears in this area.

I learned my lesson – stick to the main highway and follow a proper leader, someone who knows where he is going. We didn't have a clue! We are lucky to be alive! Thank the LORD! Mother and Dad were angry.

Mother said, "Well, you're not going to play Daniel Boone again, are you?"

No, ma'am.

I went back to my old neighborhood a couple of times, in 1992 and 1997. Nothing is the same. Gone are the old maple trees that shaded the front porch and the empty lot behind our house. The empty lot is no more; there is a house built on it. The empty lot that used to be the garbage dump now has a house built on it also. Streets are quiet, no kids. Our old house is no longer stucco, but siding, apparently aluminum. The borough paved the alley and is now a named "street," rather than just an alley, as we thought. When we lived there, it was dirt. Cars used to race up Shepherd Street, to the alley, taking a shortcut back to the main road. They did this to beat slow traffic on the steep Fourth Street hill, usually a truck or bus. The alley was very dusty, especially in the summer. With windows open to catch any breeze, we caught a lot of dust due to the cars racing up the alley to beat the traffic on the Route 88 highway.

In wandering through Charleroi and Lock Four, I was amazed how quiet and serene the town was. Also, that half the stores in the main shopping area were boarded up. There was a new Walmart across the railroad tracks, near the river. People claimed that Walmart took away a lot of the business that used to be on McKean and Fallowfield Avenues. Movie houses were no more. Charleroi used to have three or four movie houses. I think I remember only one – the Coyle – remaining.

I asked people why we saw no children, and everything was so quiet, neat and pristine in the formerly noisy neighborhood. People told me that since the mills and mines have shut down, people had to go elsewhere to find jobs. Most went to Pittsburgh and Wheeling.

Charleroi is now drafting a preservation plan to save the old buildings, which is most of the town.

High School Years
1949 TO 1952

Growing up in Lock 4, our grade school included grades One through Eight. We had no kindergarten and no junior high school. Charleroi grade schools were grades One through Six, and junior high schools were grades Seven, Eight and Nine. When I graduated from eighth grade in 1948, we kids from Lock 4 attended a junior high in Charleroi for one year – 1948-1949; then transferred to high school for grades ten through twelve.

In high school, I belonged to the Casting Club. We went to a local lake where large colored rings floated on the surface. We casted, aiming for certain targets. It was great fun. I was pretty good. I also was the only girl in the club.

In high school we were all sports fans – Charleroi High School had the best football and basketball teams in the valley. Only Monessen, across the river, was a big competitor. We kids went to every game, except away games. I played girls' softball, as catcher, pitcher and first base and sometimes shortstop. The school held dances in our huge gymnasium. We didn't need dates, but a bunch of us girls would go together. If we got to dance with a boy, so much the better, but most boys didn't want to dance. We just had fun. I wasn't allowed to date until I was sixteen anyhow, but that was OK.

I participated in the usual student activities, attending basketball and football games. We had the best sports teams around. Rab Currie, the football coach, managed to recruit players from who knows where, but we were practically unbeatable. Charleroi was a rip-roaring football and basketball town. Only Monessen, across the river, could be termed a great rival. I dated a few of the sports heroes though the relationships never lasted. It was fun while it lasted though.

I played the piano for some choral groups, even the a cappella choir for their practice sessions. These groups were good. (A cappella means "without music" or "chapel style.") I joined Tri-Hi-Y, which was organized to promote high standards of moral character in High Schools.

I had my first job while still in junior high at the age of 14, clerking at the local candy store, Gene & Boots. They made their candies on the premises, and I had to learn to wrap customers' boxes of candies professionally. I also got to work in the candy-making facility on the second floor where candies were coated with chocolate on a beltway. Fascinating to watch. One of my jobs was to test each box of chocolate covered cherries. Cherries were coated with chocolate, then have to sit for several weeks as the juicy interiors "ripen." These boxes of cherries could not be put out for sale until the centers were liquid enough. It was my job to test them. One bite out of each lot, and pretty soon I no longer wanted to see another chocolate covered cherry.

A New Home 1952

When I graduated from high school on June 3, 1952, Dad was on his way to Abilene for a reunion with his brothers. The Charleroi Mail Newspaper that morning mentioned that my father, Earl, was on his way to Abilene for festivities honoring his brother Dwight. Mother, Buddy and I drove Dad to the airport very early that morning. Consequently, he was not present for my graduation. My brother and mother were there for my graduation, along with some family friends.

My consolation was that I received a double orchid corsage from Uncle Ike and Aunt Mamie for my graduation.

In 1952 new owners who wanted to renovate our house and the duplex next door made us move since renovation would be extensive. The building needed it, as Mr. Wise, our landlord, didn't want to raise rents during the depression and war years. Consequently, no upkeep was ever done. He knew most people were on very limited incomes. Consequently, he spent no money on upkeep.

We moved to a two-story home on Liberty Avenue, down near the river, next to the railroad tracks, about 30 feet away from the tracks. It was torn down years ago. It was noisy at first, but we got used to the trains across the street and the boats on the river.

Investigating the cellar of this old house, Dad discovered a doorway, opened it and found an old root cellar, which was solidly packed dirt, as root cellars were. Looking further, he and some other men in the neighborhood found a barrel. Not knowing what was in the barrel, he and the men managed to roll the barrel up the cellar steps to the yard. Upon opening the barrel, they discovered pure whiskey. Dipping cups into the whiskey they all proclaimed it was the best whiskey they had in years, probably left over from Prohibition years. The party began – all the men standing around the barrel dipping their cups and the women on the back porches admonishing the men to be careful. I remember the scene – it was truly hilarious! How often do you find a whole barrel full of whiskey and good stuff at that? It was truly a "belly up to the barrel" moment. I certainly got none. I don't know how long the barrel lasted, or what happened to it.

We were in this house for only two years until 1954. Dad took a job in the Chicago area in 1952 or 1953. He had started working there and commuting back home every other weekend until Buddy graduated from high school in 1954. And I was commuting to and from Penn State via airline.

More Miracles – Summer 1953

In the summer of 1953 I was working as a lab technician at the Charleroi-Monessen Hospital up on the hill in North Charleroi. It was straight up the hill from where we now lived. It was quite a climb. July 4 through July 7, 1953, the period tied the all-time streak for 100-degree temperatures according to the National Weather Service. Everyone was very hot and sweaty, and no one had air conditioning in those days. Patients in the hospital were miserable, also. Even the streets and sidewalks buckled due to the heat. I was miserable, too. A group of us from the lab had been to Redd's Beach, a local swimming place, a few days before. The water there was polluted; it's amazing they were allowed to stay open. But, this day, at work I was more miserable than ever, and my throat was very sore. Attributing it to my usual allergies, I just kept on going. Finally, Mother convinced me to see Dr. Miksch, our family doctor, which I did, after work that day.

He took one look at me, gave me some pills to take and said, "Go home and go to bed."

That was it. I went home and went to bed. The next day I got out of bed and managed to drag myself up the hill to the hospital.

The doctor met me walking down the hallway and bellowed at me, "What are you doing here? (His language was *much* stronger than that.) You get yourself down the hill and to bed. I'll be by to see you this afternoon."

He came by, so did the other doctor, Senior Partner Dr. Sickman. My fever was raging. They gave me enough Penicillin to kill a horse, so to speak, and the fever raged through the Penicillin and kept on going.

Dr. Sickman stood at the foot of my bed, wagged his head back and forth and gloomily intoned, "There's nothing more we can do for Kaye."

It was one of my few lucid moments. The next day Dr. Sickman came by again. He reached into his coat pocket and pulled out some tiny, green, round ball-shaped pills. He said that a drug rep had been in his office that morning and gave him these samples. They were Chloromycetin. I managed to swallow some and the next day my fever began to break. I am lucky to be alive. Doctors advised me to take it easy for the next few weeks, not knowing what damage the strep infection might have done to my internal organs.

Other people also got the strep throat from the same source. Some survived, but some died; I don't know how many. I also learned that Chloromycetin was taken off the market as a drug to kill germs. It is apparently still used for cancer treatment.

Miracles abound! I'm still here!

Working in the lab was a great experience – the technicians there were the greatest, and everyone was a big help to me. I even got to watch autopsies. Fascinating. What a great bunch – Shirley, Joe, Leo, Bill, Gilda – we usually went to Redd's Beach after work, and once that I know of to Mineral Beach.

My job was to collect blood and urine samples from newly admitted patients, starting at 5:00 a.m. I had been taught the fine art of phlebotomy by the lab staff, then had to practice on them before they sent me forth to the patients. I got to meet everyone in the hospital – doctors, nurses, patients, volunteers (of which my mother was one), janitors, etc. One patient I went to one morning was lying stark naked on his bed covered with sores of some kind. Not knowing what his problem might be, I did not touch him (the sores looked much like syphilis sores). I went back to the lab and handed my tray and instruments to one of the guys and told him I wasn't going to touch that fellow. Apparently the patient's sores were not syphilis, but I was not a professional to be able to determine that.

It was very interesting working in a lab full-time. I only worked there two summers– 1952 and 1953. In1954 we had moved to La Grange.

The Journalists
1953

A journalist from a national magazine showed up one day. It was the summer 1953. My parents had given him the right to write an article on me. He was writing for a national magazine of good repute. (I think it was American Magazine) I was a teenager at the time. I had just finished my freshman year in college. I was so irritated at that fellow – he was dragging me all over town to get good shots, and posing me playing golf. I was not a golfer and told him so in no uncertain language. I told him he should be photographing my brother, not me. My brother was the golfer – he was a caddy at the local country club and consequently got to play golf quite a bit. He was a good golfer. The fellow wanted to know where there was a "scenic" overlook in Charleroi. No such thing – this was a mill town! I took him to the top of the local slag dump. It was a good overlook, but hardly "scenic." But, nevertheless, the writer posed me swinging a club, which I didn't know what I was doing. When the magazine published it, it featured a huge picture of me in Technicolor swinging a golf club like I knew what I was doing.

He also wanted a picture of me at work. I worked in the lab at the local hospital – the Charleroi-Monessen Hospital, on top of the hill. I told him bluntly that wouldn't be possible as we were very busy, and that was not something I could grant. Didn't bother him. He went directly to the Hospital Administrator, who eagerly gave him permission to take pictures of me at work. When I got to work, the whole lab had been rearranged to provide the photographer the best angles. I was furious that the administrator had turned lab schedule upside down to accommodate this idiot. The article published featured me as someone important, when in reality I was a lowly trainee.

Another author showed up about 1953. He had an authorization from the Eisenhower brothers to write a book on their lives. One stipulation was that he would spend time with each family, getting to know them, before writing about them. His name was (I don't want to reveal his name), from Hungary, in my estimation one of the worst writers ever. He stayed with us for I don't know how long. Must have driven mother crazy. He was rude and intrusive. When he finished his manuscript, he submitted it to Uncle Milton, who apparently had editing privileges and final say before submitting it to the publisher. Uncle Milton told me personally he had never seen such bad writing ever. Uncle Milton had to rewrite the entire manuscript to keep from embarrassing (the writer). That event was truly an intrusion into our lives. Our house was not big. We had to reshuffle everything to accommodate him.

Move to Chicago
1954

Because Dwight's brothers vowed to support him when he chose to run for President, Dad's life became more hectic than usual. Constantly called on to appear at one event or another, it became a drain on his financial resources. That is why he found another job in the Chicago area, and we moved there in 1954 after Buddy graduated from high school.

Dwight told Dad that there were jobs available in the Washington, D.C. area, so Dad went down there to investigate. The you-know-what hit the fan. Seems like every journalist in the D.C. area pictured my father's job-hunting experience as if it were graft or nepotism. Dad decided to bow out of the Washington scene, and eventually ended up managing a newspaper in the Chicago area.

Starting in 1952 Dad often had to go out in the evening to put in an appearance somewhere, what we called the "rubber chicken circuit."

He would approach me and say, "Kaye, your mother is under the weather. Would you like to go with me tonight?"

Always game for most anything, my answer was always, "Sure, Dad!"

That got me started on the political circuit. (Though I was unaware at the time, my mother was an alcoholic – details below) I learned poise and manners in front of numerous people – veterans and press. We Eisenhowers had long ago learned to "mind our manners" and always be ready for the photographers. You never knew when a photographer would pop up from who knows where? As I got older and developed the habit of smoking and drinking, one of the commandments of being an Eisenhower was, "If the Press Corps shows up, hide your drinks and cigarettes." It was considered quite unseemly to be photographed with a drink or cigarette in hand, or worse, both. We became quite adept at hiding such items. When we heard anyone in our group yell, "the press are here," we knew what to do. When we had family reunions, my female cousins and I usually hid in the ladies' room. We let my brother, Earl, Jr., and my cousin Bud, Milton, Jr., do the talking with the reporters. They did an excellent job, but I wanted nothing to do with standing before their cameras.

After we moved to Chicago (La Grange), I then had to start commuting to Penn State via airline. Flying then was exciting. I also got to cut the ribbon re-opening the small airport at Black Moshannon Airport near Penn State. That meant I didn't have to endure the long bus ride into Pittsburg to catch a plane to Chicago. Apparently it was Allegheny Airlines that handled the flights from there into Pittsburgh. It was a puddle jumper airport, as I remember a grass airfield, and flying probably at about 10,000 feet where one could see everything. We also could catch a lot of wind and weather at this altitude. It's now called the Mid-State Regional Airport near Phillipsburg.

Inauguration of Dwight David Eisenhower JANUARY 1953 (my third major trip)

(In the family Bible, his name is listed as David Dwight, but everyone called him "Dwight" because his father's name was David also. In later years, Dwight would list his name as "Dwight David.")

The incoming president decides who will get invitations to all the special events – weeklong celebrations culminating in his taking the oath of office, and the Inaugural Balls. All activities had separate invitations sent to the designated lists of people. Since we were family, we got invitations to everything. Special friends of the President got invitations. Heads of governments got theirs. Republican Governors, and ranking Republican Party workers got invitations. All Members of Congress received invitations. I still have both of my Inaugural Invitations, somewhere, from both 1953 and 1957.

Washington D.C. was a crush of people. We Eisenhowers did not have to worry about hailing a cab. The Inaugural Committee provided limousines for us, along with special drivers, who I believe were Secret Service. There were a lot of limousines as we were a large family. Children were provided separate limousines from their parents. What a blast that was. When the adults were driven off to a special function, reception, or whatever, we kids ordered our drivers to take us where we wanted to go. We went to George Washington's Home, Thomas Jefferson's Home, the Smithsonian, a session of Congress (to see how it works – or not), and the Washington Monument. We took the elevator up the Washington Monument, but decided to walk down. That was a mistake – never again!

We got to see a lot of Washington D.C. Visiting these memorable sites gave us all a sense of history. Many years later I would have chances to return and visit more places.

(In later years many more monuments, memorials and museums would be added to the list. More Smithsonian museums, the Korean and Vietnam memorials, the FDR Memorial, the WWII Memorial, all of which, except for some of the Smithsonian institutions I would have chances to see on subsequent trips.)

The first order of business was to get established in the hotel. All of the Eisenhower family was on the same floor, along with Dwight and Mamie, Johnny and Barbara and their family. The floors above and below us were unoccupied for security reasons. Each family had their suite.

One of my favorite memories is of little David Eisenhower, (Dwight's grandson and named after his great-grandfather), and Julie Nixon, Richard Nixon's daughter. They both were about six years old and became attached to each other and inseparable. It was so cute to see them on the elevators or in the hallway, walking hand in hand, two very well behaved children. We got to meet Pat and Richard Nixon, mostly coming and going in the hallways or elevators. I liked Pat; she was a warm and generous person.

We had to have plenty of clothes to last a week, for all kinds of special occasions – cocktail dresses, formal gowns, dressy street clothes, etc. However, Aunt Louise, Arthur's wife took that to the extreme. She and Arthur rented a separate suite just to accommodate all Louise's clothes. She had four or five wardrobe trunks just for her hats alone! There were additional trunks for other clothes and necessary items.

Louise paid for a special masseuse whom we all got to use. We had to sign up so there would be some order to this organized chaos! Having your personal masseuse was wonderful.

Many events were too numerous to remember specifically. Some were held in the Capitol Rotunda, which holds hundreds of people. Other events were in the largest hotels in Washington D.C. I got to meet and shake hands with just about every important person in town. I wondered how some Congressmen got elected, so boorish they were. The crush of people was never ending.

We had our Secret Service men to usher us along. Otherwise, we would have gotten lost in the crowds of people.

We had a luncheon in one of the largest hotels. The first course was oysters on the half shell. I had never seen such a thing to eat. I had always been taught to eat everything that was put in front of me, however, this plate of ugly stuff I had no idea how to attack! I watched others and asked someone beside me. Most people were eagerly downing these gooey-looking monsters. I was told to douse them with the tomato-based sauce that came with the plates of food. I managed to get perhaps six or so down before I finally quit. At first, I was trying to chew them, and then someone informed me that you swallow them whole! That would have been easier to swallow. Sorry, folks,

I'm not going to finish the rest. I made a game try. That was enough!

At this same luncheon, drinks were ordered all around, and Uncle Ed, bless his heart, ordered a Martini for me. I had taken a couple sips, but no more. (At home when we were growing up, Dad and Mom would give us kids, when we were teenagers, small glasses of wine, to teach us how to drink wine. You don't gulp it, like water! You sip alcoholic drinks.) Dad came late to the seating and saw the Martini sitting in front of me. He blew his stack! Asking how in the world I got such a drink, Ed owned up. Boy, did Dad ream him out. I then got a soda to drink, and the Martini taken away. Darn! The drinking age was 21, but I was only 18 at the time.

One luncheon was in the Capital Rotunda. It holds an enormous number of people. I believe there were perhaps 200 people or even more. At the beginning of our country, church services for government employees and officials were held here. It is a very historic place, and I couldn't help gawking around to see as much as possible of this historic site.

There was a prayer service at the National Cathedral, with Dwight and Mamie and the rest of our families sitting in the front rows just prior to the swearing-in ceremony.

Inauguration Day was cold and fairly clear. President Truman and incoming President Eisenhower rode in separate cars to the ceremony.

In past years, the outgoing and incoming presidents would ride in the same car. Truman and Eisenhower had a falling out about the time of Uncle Ike's barnstorming campaign. Their spat has different reasons, but the biggest reason, I believe, is that both the Democrats and Republicans were wooing Uncle Ike to run for President on their ticket. Both Democrats and Republicans made trips to Paris, where Uncle Ike then was heading up NATO. He had to give their issues a lot of thought and much discussion with his brothers. Harry Truman worked hard to get Uncle Ike to run on the Democratic ticket. They had worked well together during the War, and perhaps Truman expected Dwight would go Democrat. When he decided to run on the Republican ticket, the friendship blew up. They never reconciled. Uncle Ike also decided to wear a Homburg, rather than the traditional Top Hat. Some people were not happy with that; tradition being what it is in Washington DC.

During the inauguration ceremony, Dwight's brothers and their wives were seated on the balcony with him and the Supreme Court Justices. He took the oath of office on the Bible his parents had given him while he was at West Point. It was a standard King James version. During the ceremony, Uncle Ike said a brief prayer, which he had composed himself:

> *"Almighty God*
>
> *As we stand here at this moment, my future associates in the executive branch of the Government join me in beseeching that Thou will make full and complete our dedication to the service of the people in this throng and their fellow citizens everywhere.*
>
> *Give us, we pray, the power to discern clearly right from wrong and allow all our words and actions to be governed thereby and by the laws of this land.*
>
> *Especially we pray that our concern shall be for all the people, regardless of station, race or calling.*
>
> *May cooperation be permitted and be the mutual aim of those who, under the concept of our Constitution, hold to differing political beliefs – so that all may work for the good of our beloved country and for Thy Glory*
>
> *Amen"*

During the Inaugural Ceremony, all of us cousins were seated down front in the first row of bleacher seats, facing up at our parents. Behind us in the second row was the press corps. One of the press people behind us made the comment, "Who's the (lady) in the orange coat?" (However, the language the press corps people used was much more graphic than that.)

We kids just about came unglued. The actual words said were more of an epithet. It was hard to maintain decorum. Our parents warned us that we had to behave because we were Eisenhowers! The orange coat person was my aunt, up to her antics as usual, doing her darnedest to be the center of attention. With the bright orange coat, dyed black hair and white complexion, she was a sight to behold! Amid the sea of dark suits and dress coats, the bright orange outfit did stand out!

There were, to my recollection, three Inaugural Balls. There may have been more. The whole family had to go to all three, and of course we had to dance at each one. We would enter the ballroom, make our appearances, dance one or two dances and leave for the next Ball.

While we were in Washington and visiting the White House, Aunt Mamie gave us a guided tour of the whole White House, bottom to top. We got to see rooms and places the usual visitors don't ever see. One collection we got to see was the china collection from past presidents. We also saw every single room – Red Room, Blue Room, Green Room, State Dining Room, Oval Office, then to the upper stories where the bedrooms are. We got to see Lincoln's bedroom, and the family quarters, always off limits to the public. There is so much history in The White House. It was fascinating to me. We got to spend some time in the family quarters.

When we were checking out of the hotel at the end of the week's festivities, Dad went up to the clerk, only to be told that his bill was already paid. I would only guess that Uncle Ed probably paid. He was making so much money he was giving it away because he said the government was taking 90% of his income anyway.

Apple Blossom Festival
1953

Uncle Milton was a surrogate father to me. He was much like my father. One day he called me to his study and I'm wondering, "What did I do now?" However, this time was different. It seems that the Committee to Select the 1953 Apple Blossom Queen had determined that I was a likely candidate for that position. My parents had approved, they notified Uncle Milton, and it was Uncle Milton's job to put the question to me.

Did I want to accept it? I'm pretty game for anything, so I said "yes." I had no idea what was entailed, but I would soon find out.

I did learn that in the weeks prior to the Committee selecting me, they had a squad of people following me around campus. I had no idea of this surveillance. Can you imagine someone following you around for days and having not a clue?

Eventually, I learned that there was one criterion to be the Apple Blossom Queen. One had to be related to someone famous. With my uncle in the White House, I guess that made me eligible. I did not have to be bright, talented, or beautiful and all that stuff, as so many pageants are. However, it appeared that the Committee wanted someone with decorum and good manners. Apparently, that is why they followed me around campus.

Once I made the decision, I was given the criteria for dress code for each event. I would need cocktail dresses, street dresses, etc. for different affairs. It was all quite specific. Luckily, I had some formal dresses from my high school days. One thing most important was the selection of the gown I would need for the final day of the parade and my inauguration as Apple Blossom Queen on the steps of Handley High School. It had to be a long white gown, with a train and lace, long sleeved, with high bosom, in other words, like an expensive wedding gown.

Ouch! Stuff like that costs money! Poor Dad. Dad, however, was not undone. In Charleroi, there was a dress shop named Zelinski's. The owner, Mrs. Zelinski, whom everyone called "Madam Z," was a skillful proprietor. Dad approached her with a deal. If he could get such a wedding-type gown for a reduced rate, he would allow Madam

Z to display my dresses in her shop window after the Apple Blossom Festival was over. It was a done deal. My Apple Blossom Wardrobe was displayed in her window after we got home, and I had the precious white gown needed for the Apple Blossom Inauguration festivities.

I learned that an elderly couple, my chaperones, would be driving me to Winchester, Virginia, from Penn State. They were probably middle-aged – perhaps in their 40s, but at my age, anyone over 30 was old. I would meet my parents and brother there. Sadly, I've forgotten their names. When the cities of Berkeley Springs and Martinsburg, West Virginia learned that our route to Winchester was near them, they requested that I make personal appearances in their cities. We did that, and both cities presented me with keys to their cities. Celebrations in each city ensued, with the required pictures in the national newspapers. The keys to the two cities still hang on my wall. They are carved wood, about three feet long, so their wall space is quite prominent.

Keys to the cities of Berkeley Springs
and Martinsburg, West Virginia

The day of the final event, the official parade and inauguration, was April 29, Mom and Dad's 20th wedding anniversary. How auspicious is that?

Upon arriving in Winchester, where every year since forever the Apple Blossom Festival has been held, I was installed in Senator Byrd's home. It was a magnificent mansion, befitting one of the most powerful senators in Virginia. He was the elder Senator Byrd, not the younger who was currently in Congress. The Black Negro maids waited on me hand and foot. I could not even dress myself, nor change clothes. The maids, dressed in black uniforms with white aprons and little white caps on their heads, were throughout the house.

The ones assigned to me did everything for me. I was thoroughly spoiled. I could get used to being spoiled.

The doyennes of Winchester society put on this annual affair since forever, and they did it to perfection. Never did I ever see an event of this magnitude move along so smoothly. The ladies who graced these beautiful mansions were the most graceful and charming people I've ever met. Their graciousness and hospitality were the epitomai of the old-fashioned "Southern Hospitality!"

The Apple Blossom Festival events lasted for a whole week, culminating in the Coronation and Grand Parade on Friday. Every day, there were luncheons, dinners, dances, and on and on. I had a different escort for every affair. I got to know some of my escorts, and after the Apple Blossom Festival was over, I dated a couple of them - one from West Virginia U and one from Colgate. We had some great times.

The Event Committee typed up the schedule for each day's events. They would then distribute the schedule to all the event participants. It was quite detailed as to exact times, down to the minute, for appearances, meals, broadcasts, interviews, dances, etc. It was worthy of a schedule for the

President of the United States, who submits to such a schedule daily.

Apple Blossom Committee – permission granted by the Apple Blossom Committee

The Parade float – on board with me are my two Maids, Ann Arthur and Diane Hunt

Apple Blossom Committee – permission granted by the Apple Blossom Committee

General Van Fleet officially crowning me as Apple Blossom Queen Shenandoah XXVI. The culmination of festivities was the crowning of the Apple Blossom Queen. I was crowned officially on April 29, 1953, on the steps of Handley High School.

Apple Blossom Committee – permission granted by the Apple Blossom Committee

Here, we are watching the Apple Blossom Pageant. My brother Earl Jr. (Bud), Mother and Dad are in the foreground on the left of the viewing platform. I'm on the queen's seat on the viewing platform with Maids Ann Arthur and Diane Hunt.

Permission given by the Apple Blossom Committee

Original painting by Milton Caniff of me painted expressly for the Apple Blossom Festival publicity. Milton Caniff was the famous cartoonist and author of *Terry and the Pirates* and *Steve Canyon* comic strips.

There were many other celebrities taking part in the Pageant and Festival events: Grand Marshal Arthur Godfrey, Milton Caniff, William (Hopalong Cassidy) Boyd, Joe Kirkwood (famous trickshot golfer), Jackson Weaver, Frank Hardin, Luci Miller and Mary Jane Bridenbaugh.

Sometime in the spring of 1953 I was invited to be the Cotton Queen in Altoona, Pennsylvania. I was not crazy about going, but adults around me felt it would be good, so I went. More pictures in the papers. However, this time, I don't remember all kinds of fancy balls, clothes, etc. I think it was something of a one-day affair, but nevertheless I did miss a day or two of school. My professors, by this time, were probably tired of seeing me excused from classes so many times.

The grand event being over, it was time to return to college life. I had missed several classes and found it difficult to catch up. By the end of the semester, I failed a class. Bummer! There went part of my summer to take a makeup class. But I struggled through.

College Life
1952-1955

In the fall of 1952 I enrolled at Penn State. It was then Penn State College. A year or so later the named changed to Pennsylvania State University. I still have a sweatshirt with the "State College" logo. Campus life was a new world, as it is to every incoming freshman.

Our first week was orientation. We got to know our roommates and other girls in our dorm. We were taken from one place to another on campus to orient us to the campus and facilities. We got to know the dorm, the House Mother, the rules and regulations, and facilities within the dorm and on campus. While doing this, I begged my roommate to NOT tell others what my last name was. I wanted to find out who my friends were first. My roommate, Judy, was very good at that, and I was always grateful to her.

However, one night, before "lights out," eight or nine of us were gathered in one of the rooms, sitting around drinking hot chocolate or coffee. Yes, we did have "lights out" and bed checks after 10:00 p.m. One of the girls exclaimed, "I heard that there is an Eisenhower girl on campus who was found dead drunk at a local fraternity house and had to be brought back to the dorm by the campus cops." I almost burst out laughing and had to leave the room before I split my side. Judy left with me. Out in the hallway, we let it loose and laughed until we couldn't laugh anymore. First, I had never been to a fraternity house, secondly had never had an alcoholic drink on campus, and thirdly had never been drunk in my life. I realized then that people would criticize and gossip about me no matter what I did. From then on I decided to live my life and let the chips fall where they may. I figured my friends would know what I was like, and for others, I didn't care what they thought. Gossip can be a wicked thing if you cave into it.

Centrally located between Old Main and the HUB Student Center, the McAllister Building is now the home of the Department of Mathematics at Penn State. Mac Hall was constructed in 1904, and originally occupied as a men's dormitory. In 1915, it became a women's dormitory and was later converted to an academic building. In addition to the Math Department, the McAllister

Building also houses the on-campus U.S. Post Office, which is the official home of the zip code 16802 (University Park).

When I was at Penn State, McAllister Hall, was a freshman women's dorm. It was directly across the compound from Old Main and the Student Union.

When I was at Penn State, there were acres of green campus between buildings. I was so disappointed to see the campus in later years almost totally built out, stuffed with buildings. It is so different from the bucolic years of the early 1950s. The Creamery, for instance, was on the north side of campus, just a few minutes walk from our dorm. We used to walk over there on Sundays to get a freshly made ice cream cone, or perhaps a jug of fresh cider.

I was walking with some friends across campus one day when we met a bunch of kids coming our way. We all stopped to greet each other – my friends knew the kids who approached us, but I did not. One of them introduced me, saying, "I'd like you to meet Kaye Eisenhower."

As with one voice, they responded, almost breathlessly, "You said 'Kaye E-I-S-E-N-H-O-W-E-R?'"

I couldn't believe my ears. These people were ready to fall at my feet because I was an Eisenhower. I never did anything famous. It was my uncle who deserved all the fame. I had long ago learned to be very pragmatic about being an Eisenhower. Yes, there are perks, so to speak, but I was not the famous one!!! I had to learn that the star power, the light from Uncle Ike's star fell on the rest of the family. Every member of the family was affected in different ways: one became a publicity hound; others turned to alcohol; some accepted the fame that came their way; others tried to escape it.

November 1952

It was election night, 1952. Our housemother, bless her, allowed us to forego the usual lights out commandment and stay up listening to the latest election returns since by now everyone in the dorm knew I was Kaye Eisenhower. Of course, because of that, everyone was interested. I can't imagine any other time in history when college freshmen would be interested in election night returns. It was an uproarious celebration when Uncle Ike won. The noise and jubilation carried on for hours, or for as long as we could get away with it.

The Jug of Cider

Sometime in the fall, my roommate Judy and I had bought a gallon jug of cider at the creamery north of the campus. Fresh cider was a real treat. However, it was impossible to drink it all, even sharing with friends. We left the remainder, almost half a jug, on the windowsill of the dorm.

The walls of this dorm, the oldest dorm on campus, were about two or three feet wide and solid stone. The windowsill made an excellent refrigeration unit in the fall and winter. Draperies covered the window, and our desks, facing each other, abutted the window. Since the weather was becoming colder, we had left the draperies closed, the window cracked a bit and forgot about the cider. We would leave the window cracked open a bit for fresh air.

One night we went out and upon returning and opening the door to our room, the pungent odor of whisky overpowered us. Not knowing what happened, we investigated and discovered that the bottle of cider was on the floor in pieces, and the contents scattered across the room. The wind rolled the jug across our desks and crashed on the floor, where it broke into pieces, creating the odoriferous whisky smell.

Just about that time, the House Mother showed up at our doorway. She smelled the obvious, looked at me (why not Judy also?) and said in a very sad and dolorous voice, "Oh, Kaye!"

I had to explain to her that it was a jug of cider, which was easy to see, as we had not the time yet to clean it up. She believed me. I wonder if she would have believed anyone else. I seemed to be her pet and could do no wrong. I took advantage of that and got away with many shenanigans, as a result.

Yes, cider does become whisky if you let it sit long enough.

The Water Fun

Sometime later that semester, the girls in our hallway got crazy, and we decided to have water fights – water balloons, fixing buckets of water over doorways to spill when the door opened, etc. We had water everywhere. It was a sloppy mess. Nearing 10:00 PM, someone saw or heard the Housemother coming, and it was a "cheez-it, the cops" moment. As we tried to scatter to our rooms and pretend all was well, one of the girls slipped on some water, cracked her head and was out cold. Jeez – what do we do now? Too late, the Housemother caught us and we were all in trouble.

I don't remember what the punishment was, but we did have to clean up all the mess we made. We had water from one end of the hallway to the other. Luckily, the girl who was knocked out came to and appeared to be OK, fortunately.

The antics never ended. What do you expect with a bunch of teenage girls? One never knew when her bed might be short-sheeted, or going to bed at night, someone would come into your room with a pan of warm water and put your hand in the pan. I lost count of the number who wet their beds, as a result. Very embarrassing.

Fraternity Parties

There were fraternity parties every Friday and Saturday night, but the big blowouts occurred during special times of the year. One big event would be the annual spring party where the house seniors dictated what the "drink of the day" would be. One affair I went to with my date, Ed, the seniors had decreed that the drink of the day would be grain alcohol and orange juice. When Ed and I got there, it was quite warm for a spring day, and everyone was hot and thirsty, consequently drinking more than usual. The orange juice/ alcohol punch tasted just like orange juice and I was drinking my share. Ed kept telling me to slow down, that that drink could be potent. By that time, it probably didn't matter much. I was becoming unsteady on my feet, to say the least. Ed made me walk around the block several times until he felt that I could walk on my own. Bless him! When we got back to the fraternity house, there was not a soul in an erect position. Throughout the entire house, Ed and I walked, in an out of every bedroom and dormitory, living room, every room. Not a soul awake. Everyone – all the guys and their dates zonked out. Pretty scary! I'm glad Ed had the guts to walk me around the block until I was sober.

At another fraternity party, we dates were given one yard of floral material for making a costume for their annual luau party. The one yard of material barely covered the necessary parts, but all us girls were dressed alike – in sarongs a la Dorothy Lamour! The sarongs covered about what a bathing suit would cover, so it wasn't too bad. Thank Heavens bikinis hadn't hit the big scene yet.

Other big fraternities held many parties during football season. Penn State was big on football, and coach Joe Paterno had led the team to some stupendous victories. Consequently, football weekends were big weekends for celebrating, with more drinking than usual.

One time a bunch of us went to Philadelphia to attend the big Penn State/Penn game. Penn was one of our biggest rivals, and always a cause for bigger parties than usual. Our first stop was at a hotel where we were meeting a bunch of other kids, and I was tagging along because I had never done this before. When we got to the hotel room, it had a main gathering room with bedrooms on either side. Guys were passing around a warm bottle of booze, of which everyone was freely partaking. Girls and guys were slipping off to the adjacent bedrooms. I perceived this to not be a ball game, but a drinking/sex party. So thoroughly disgusted with this scene, I walked out of the hotel without telling anyone, asked the doorman the way to the train station, then walked by myself all the way to the train station. I got off at Bryn Mawr, then had to call a taxi to get to the house where we all were staying.

I went to Pittsburgh one weekend for the big Penn State/Pitt game, the other major rival of Penn State. That game was ALWAYS the weekend before Thanksgiving. Strict campus rules said we had to be back in our dorms at 10:00 PM Sunday evening and professors would severely punish anyone missing Monday class. A doggone shame, as Pittsburgh was so close to home. Dad would be driving to Penn State on Thursday to pick me up.

One weekend Penn State played West Virginia. My date was from West Virginia, so I sat with him in the West Virginia section. Much to my chagrin, I didn't dare root for Penn State sitting in that section, but we had fun, anyway.

Uncle Milton had tried very hard to make Penn State a dry campus, but after a few years there, I could tell it wasn't going to happen. Penn State's reputation as "The Party School of the East" would stand for many more years. When at a fraternity, I always nursed a mug of beer all evening, determined not to get drunk. With a name like Eisenhower, getting drunk would create a lot of gossip. My friends knew what I was like, so gossip didn't bother me.

At other times, usually around Thanksgiving, bunches of boys and girls would fly to Havana over the holiday weekend. When I called Dad to see if I could go, thinking this could be fun, his response was a big "NO!" I learned later that the girls were bunking about a dozen or more to each room. I'm glad I didn't go. However, seeing Havana before Castro took over might have been rather exotic.

Ice Skating

One of the most fun things I learned at Penn State was the art of ice skating. When we first were there, the only ice skating was at a lake north of campus. We would shovel the snow off the ice, and then out in the middle of the lake we built a fire to roast marshmallows or whatever we were roasting that evening. That was such fun. It was always cold at Penn State in the winter and usually plenty of snow. Later, perhaps a year or so, Penn State built an ice rink on the east end of campus near where the veterans' housing was.

After that, we didn't have to drive out to the lake because the rink was so convenient.

As an afterthought, our senior dorm (I think it was McKean) overlooked the veterans' housing on the east end of campus at that time. It was pathetic. The wives would come out early in the morning to a community pump to pump water needed for their family. I think it was mostly couples. I don't remember children. The housing was terrible, shacks, all lined up next to each other like one long barrack. I hope the school eventually built better housing for veterans.

All these escapades might make it seem like campus life was one big party. It wasn't! I had classes six days a week and heavy duty homework almost every evening. My poor brain could get so befuddled, especially when trying to conquer quantitative analysis. Quantitative analysis blew me out of school, too. All I could think of was there had to be a better way to make a living!

Campus Life Spring 1953
Cousins Ruth and Bud

Uncle Milton had a mansion on campus, and I used to spend a lot of time there. My cousin Ruth, his daughter, and I were great friends. We shared some hilarious times together. Neither of us knew diddly squat about cooking. But in the wee hours of the morning, we would go down the back stairs to the kitchen and cook up something, leaving the kitchen an unholy mess, then go back to bed. I'll bet the cook wanted to murder us when she came to work the next morning.

When I stayed with Ruth, the maid would have fresh orange juice on a server in our rooms when we awoke. Breakfast would be served in the formal dining room once we dressed and were ready to face the day.

Cousin Bud (Milton, Jr.), Ruth's brother was around also. Being four years older and working on his Masters Degree, he was familiar with campus life and all the people at various fraternities. He was a member of SAE (Sigma Alpha Epsilon), probably one of the drinkingest frats on campus.

Penn State was supposed to be a dry campus. Yeh, right! The fraternity brothers of all the frats made regular trips on Fridays to Bellefonte for kegs of beer and much more. I can only imagine the traffic back and forth on the road to Bellefonte from State College.

Bud introduced me to numerous fellows on campus. He was my buddy, my companion and squire on campus. Some guys I met I liked, others

I did not. However, my thinking was, "I'll go out with this guy because I just may meet someone else." Nothing bothered me except the guys who thought I was an easy mark. Uh-uh! I disappointed a lot of guys.

One fellow I dated went home on holiday and told everyone in his hometown that we would be married in the White House. I found out about this fakeroo from another guy I was dating, who was from the same hometown. Boy! This scumbag was furthest down on my list!

Bud was wonderful. He squired me around campus. I got to know many of the fraternities. He had the keys to Uncle Milton's cabin in the woods and often used it for wild parties. I was along on one of these escapades and decided, "No more!" I don't think Uncle Milton knew that Bud was using the cabin for all those parties. The booze flowed freely, to say the least.

But, I thought the world of Bud. He was truly one of the greatest people I've ever known. When he died several years ago, I was sad. He was one of the world's "stand-up" guys, and many people missed him. My brother and I missed his funeral because he kept all his friends' addresses on his computer and his wife didn't know how to access the information. My brother and I found out about his death several days later, and both of us felt so bad. Bud was always one of my favorite people in this world and worthy of all the kind words said about him at his memorial service. We found out about his death through cousin Mary Jean Eisenhower, Uncle Ike's granddaughter. I still miss Bud. I miss Ruth, too. She and I were best buddies for the few years I was on campus. She died in 1984, much too young, from throat cancer. She was only 45, but she continued her life, even showing up on television to promote the projects she was supporting, until the day before she died.

Returning to Penn State in the fall of 1953 I was assigned to a sophomore dorm (McElwain). Freshmen dorms were reserved strictly for freshmen. The Sorority Rush soon started. That is when all the sororities (and fraternities as well) try to secure as many new people as possible. There are criteria for some. We had 22 sororities on campus. One had a low scholastic rating, so they needed girls with high-grade point averages. One (or maybe more, I don't remember) was a Jewish sorority. The new sophomores were free to attend as many rush parties as they wished, rather like open houses, where you attended, signed the guest list and left.

Most girls would get two or three, perhaps four or five invitations for return events. I was shocked to learn that I got invitations from 20 sororities. Didn't that tell me something? I decided to go where my friends were going – most of them went to Kappa Kappa Gamma (Kappas), Pi Beta Phi (Betas) and Kappa Alpha Theta (Thetas). Since most of my friends went to Kappa, I decided to go there too. Apparently all these sororities wanted my name more than they wanted me.

Junior/Senior Dorm 1954- 1955

I became a Pledge with KKG (Kappa Kappa Gamma) Sorority. I loved this group of girls. There were none greater on campus. In the fall of 1954 I was assigned to a Senior Dorm. We seniors were allowed some leeway in choosing the dorm we preferred. I chose this dorm because it was a Junior/Senior dorm, and the Kappa suite was in this dorm.

Sororities on the Penn State campus had suites in the Junior/Senior dorms, unlike the fraternities that had their houses scattered about town.

The Kappa suite was down the hall from my room. Life was hectic and full of events in which to participate. You participated in their events if you were a member of a sorority. My studies suffered. I found it hard to concentrate when there were constant parties or bridge games going on. That's where I learned to play bridge – a great game, but it sure cut into my study time. Even trying to study was difficult. The noise and constant interruptions from well-meaning friends were constant distractions.

All the sororities and fraternities participated in The All-Campus Sing. When we were practicing for this event, I was told to stand in the back row, to move my mouth but not utter a sound. I never could carry a tune in a bucket.

Every fall the campus elected the King and Queen from among fraternity and sorority members. It seems that a Kappa was often the Queen.

This dorm had a different housemother, and she didn't care who I was – just another one of the girls. Strict – every morning she would sit by the front door as we left to make sure we all had skirts on. The rule was that girls were NOT allowed to wear pants or jeans on campus. Skirts had to be mid-calf length.

However, I had two lab classes each week that required us to cut up cadavers (included in the third-year medical courses) that were giant cats expressly raised for medical students. They were soaked in formaldehyde. Each lesson we would cut apart a different part of the body, very similar to the human body, so we students could learn how the various parts of the human body fit together. We worked with the usual scalpels, but no rubber gloves or protective clothing. That is why I wore jeans, rolled up under my skirt. When I got to class, I removed my skirt, put on an old shirt and went to work. By the time I got back to the dorm at 5:00 PM, dinnertime, I reeked of formaldehyde. Even after taking a shower and putting on clean clothes, I still could smell that awful stuff. Dining room decorum dictated dresses, no pants for the girls and all the meals were formal, served by white-coated waiters who were boys working their way through school.

After dinner, some of us girls would get together with the waiters and play cards, often bridge and sometimes poker. Poker was not allowed – that was gambling! However, if we were playing poker, we would have to keep a watch for the housemother and quickly sweep coins or chips under the table. If she came by, we would pretend to be playing bridge.

Hurricane Hazel came blasting through Pennsylvania in the fall of 1954. It was a deadly, powerful and costly storm, the worst of the 1954 hurricane season on the Atlantic. I had been in a three-hour lab class all day and upon exiting the building the wind was blowing powerfully, so much so we found it extremely difficult to walk. I made my way to the main boulevard that crosses the campus and hung on to the trees as I ran from one to another tree to the end of campus where our dorm was. At times, as I was hanging on, the wind blew me off my feet. My umbrella was turned inside out as soon as I opened it, and the wind was so strong it was driving the rain right through my cloth raincoat. I finally arrived back at the dorm, soaking wet.

I am surprised that no one notified us that a powerful storm was coming.

Life After College

In the spring of 1955 my boyfriend and I were planning marriage. I was pinned to him for a semester or two. I dearly wanted to go with him when he went off to law school. He asked me to marry him and go with him, but for some reason, I said, "No." We split shortly afterward. I've always wondered if I made the right decision. I'll never know, but I still think about him. The past is past and cannot be undone.

Upon arriving home in La Grange Park (Chicago), I received a notice from the university that I had failed another class and was no longer welcome on campus. My university career was over.

This was a terrible time for me. What a blow! My Father said to me: "I'm not going to help you again."

I didn't blame him.

Mother looked at me and said "How can I hold up my head to my friends?"

I thought, "Lady, I don't care about your head!"

I even contemplated suicide. I felt so worthless. Sitting alone in the dark one evening thinking about how I could accomplish such an act, I heard a voice, "Kaye Eisenhower, you are worth something!" I flipped the lights on to find out who belonged to the voice, but no one was there. I had plenty of time to think.

Another miracle!

It was then I began the long climb back to normality, finding a business school (Moser) and reclaiming some self-esteem. It required hard work and discipline.

For a long time, even at Penn State, I had wanted to go into Business Administration, but the school would not let me transfer. Now I had the opportunity. I found an excellent business school – Moser Secretarial School – in downtown Chicago. They taught women not only basic business skills like typing and shorthand, but also accounting and office management. They also taught proper office clothing and business etiquette. That meant hats (yes, hats), gloves, and shoes that matched our outfits. Plus jewelry that matched our outfits.

We had to learn to type at 80 to 100 words per minute and take shorthand at 100 to 120 words per minute. We had the old manual typewriters.

Electric ones were coming into use, but our training was on the old manuals. Our typing had to be perfect – there were to be no erasures in the letters we typed. We threw a lot of paper into the wastebaskets.

When Moser's protégés were ready to hit the pavement, they were ready for almost anything. All their graduates got premium job offers around the Chicago area. Moser graduates were much in demand. We were Executive Secretaries, considered not just secretaries, but skilled office managers. I have Dr. and Mrs. Moser to thank for the managerial training I got in 1955-56. It led to a good career.

In the 1950s, men who were office managers and did the same things as the ladies who were Executive Secretaries got paid twice as much. That was life then. All of us got top offers from businesses around Chicago. My first offer was a very high paying one from a beer company. However, my family nixed that idea, as their opinion of an Eisenhower working at a beer company would not be seemly. So much for being an Eisenhower.

During the time I was attending Moser, and after I had obtained a good job at the National Safety Council, I rode the CB&Q commuter train into Chicago every day. My best friend, Barbara

Millar, and I rode together. One day we met Tom Morgan on the train. Barb had gone to school with him at Miami University in Oxford, Ohio. She introduced us, and we went back to our seats.

Later on, Tom asked Barb, "How do you find a decent girl in this town?"

That's when she decided to push us together.

It was fun riding the commuter. Everyone took the same train every evening and every morning. Groups would sit together, and some would play bridge or read newspapers. No matter how late you arrived, your seat was always waiting. It was like we all had reservations. Standees would not dare to take an empty seat until after the train started moving. We had a great society. I don't know if this custom still exists.

Sometimes on Thursday or Friday nights we would stay in Chicago and go to a different restaurant and later go to a movie or nightclub or show. Then we'd take a later train home, before midnight. Trains after midnight ran sporadically, and downtown Chicago after midnight was not a great place to be.

Tom rode the same train as Barb and I did. We had a few conversations, and he asked me for a date. It was months before I finally went out with him. After a few dates, he started pestering me to marry him. I finally caved, and we set a date of November 17, 1956. Mother and Dad were not happy, but they didn't reveal their feelings to me at the time. They did everything they could to break us up.

Uncle Ed - Tacoma
1956

Uncle Ed was the second oldest Eisenhower brother, born in January 1889, in Hope, Kansas, when Arthur, the oldest boy, was barely two years old. He, too, graduated from high school, a rarity in those days, as most kids left school after eighth grade to work the family farm. Ed always wanted to be a lawyer, and ended up going to what became Michigan State University and obtained his law degree. He always figured the life in the west was wild and untamed, so elected to go to Tacoma after graduating. He discovered that Tacoma was quite settled and entered a law firm, beginning his law career around 1910 or so. His story is told in his book, "Six Roads From Abilene," published several decades ago.

Uncle Ed was a character – raucous, always telling jokes, extremely careful with his diet – an alcoholic drink or two, but no more, and only the healthiest of foods. Daily he hung himself from the rafters of his basement in a special halter, which he claimed, "stretched his spine." He was the best golfer in the family, but that fact could never be published as long as his brother, Dwight, was President.

The two brothers (Ed and Dwight) were always extremely close all their lives, and their rivalry and companionship was famous. Uncle Ed played amateur golf up and down the west coast for years. On this 80th birthday, he scored his age, for which he got a special commendation from the golf club to which he belonged. Uncle Ed was the best senior golfer on the west coast.

Ed was famous on the west coast, and wealthy. His home in Tacoma was on American Lake, with its own dock, with a view of Mt. Rainier.

Uncle Ed had a repertoire of jokes like none other. One evening he and a bunch of his fellow businessmen and lawyers were having dinner in a restaurant in Tacoma. He told a joke about a baby bird being kicked out of the nest by mama bird. Baby bird finally learned to fly, and he flew and flew and it was getting dark and didn't know how to find his way back to his nest. He is getting scared. End of joke: Do you know how baby bird calls his mama? At this point, Ed yells loudly, "MAMA!" The joke is a real screamer if you haven't heard it before. The upshot is that the loud MAMA so startled a waiter coming through the swinging kitchen doors (near where they were sitting) with a huge load of dinners, that he dropped the whole tray of dinners all over the floor. So much for Uncle Ed. He never stopped with the jokes. I would not advise telling this joke in a crowded restaurant ever again.

I enjoyed getting to know Uncle Ed. He was such a character, and you'll never see a picture of him with his mouth closed. When Uncle Ike was President, the two of them had running political feuds going in the national newspapers. Newspapers were always glad to publish Ed's political views, quite different from Dwight's.

Uncle Ike finally had to write to Ed and say bluntly, "Please stop all the politicking out there on the west coast. I have enough trouble here in Washington."

His brothers considered Ed's politics to be right of Attila the Hun.

One of my parents' tactics was to have Uncle Ed invite me to stay with him for a month in Tacoma, Washington, where Ed was a lawyer, a very famous and successful lawyer. My parents were hoping I'd find someone else in which to become interested. Didn't work, but the trip was fun.

My trip to Tacoma started in Chicago taking the Union Pacific to Portland, Oregon. Along the way, we went through northern Illinois, then into Iowa, Nebraska, Wyoming, Montana, and Idaho. We went through a part of the Snake River valley and finally down the Columbia River Gorge into Portland. The Columbia River Valley was incredibly beautiful. I asked the porter what time we would enter the Columbia River Gorge, and he said it would be about 4:00 AM. I told him to wake me, that I didn't want to miss a bit of the River and its beauty. That trip down the Columbia was spectacular, I felt as though I couldn't take enough of it in.

Along the way, I got to see lots of sights that were part of the history of this country. The trip across the Mississippi was astounding. I couldn't imagine building a railroad bridge that would span such an expanse of water. I remember Cheyenne (and all the coal dust) and Green River, Wyoming (all coal dust). I remember the Continental Divide west of Creston, Wyoming (I expected a mountain ridge of some kind, but this land was very flat here). We saw the stockyards in Laramie, Granger, Wyoming and Pocatello, Idaho, and Omaha, Nebraska. In many of these places the train stopped, and we had a chance to get out and walk around.

During the three-day trip westward I met a group of young men, and we got to play bridge. We played bridge non-stop until we got to Portland, taking time out to eat and to retire for the night, taking up our bridge game the next morning after breakfast. Great fun. I enjoyed those fellows.

My stay in Tacoma with Uncle Ed and his wife, Lucy, was an exciting time. We traveled around the state and saw many sights – from Mt. Rainier to the Puyallup Valley to old forts. Mt. Rainier in May was snowed under, with snow up to the roof of the inn. Great tunnels dug through the snow were the only way to the inn. Snow was piled high along the highway.

We went out to dinner often. There is no greater place than the Seattle area to find good seafood, especially crab and salmon. I loved all these wonderful, scenic, magnificent restaurants. Walking the docks, we had to be careful. The boats were off-loading huge buckets of king crab, and the crabs were falling out of the buckets and wandering all over the dock.

Ed and Lucy did find some dates for me. One I'll never forget: one guy came with his regular girlfriend and I was his second. Talk about feeling like a fifth wheel! But, Ed didn't know a lot of younger folks my age. Consequently, I had few dates on this trip and spent all my time gallivanting around with Lucy and her friends, which was great fun. Lucy was vivacious and charming though Ed divorced her shortly afterward. Claimed she was a gold-digger.

On my return trip, I took the Great Northern Railroad, the Empire Builder train. This luxury train went through Northern Idaho (Coeur d'Alene), Montana (Glacier National Park), North Dakota, Minnesota, down the Mississippi and through Minneapolis/St. Paul. I remember Williston, North Dakota. The trip across the Mississippi into Northern Minnesota was not so grand as the southern crossing – the river is quite a bit smaller in Minnesota.

I arrived home in late May 1956.

Marriage
November 17, 1956

Tom and I married in November 1956 in the chapel of the Congregational Church in La Grange. Mother planned all the details and Dad paid for everything. I was glad, as both Tom and I were working full time. Mother chose the flowers and other details; Dad chose the wedding reception site. I was glad for all the help.

There were articles of my engagement in most newspapers across the country. It was 1956, and Uncle Ike had won a second term. All the articles featured me as the "niece of President and Mrs. Eisenhower." I was becoming a celebrity. My other cousins were 10 to 12 years older, married with children, and consequently not much in the publicity picture as I was.

One of the first things Tom and I had to do was to hire a bodyguard for the ceremony. How many people have to hire a bodyguard for their wedding? Tom's friend, an Okie from Oklahoma, was chosen for his expertise in handling people, both verbally and physically. During the ceremony, he was stationed outside the chapel, so no one except those on the guest list could enter. That left a lot of frustrated reporters and photographers waiting outside.

Once the ceremony was over, and the doors opened, and Tom and I emerged from the chapel to face a barrage of reporters and photographers. It was a melee. As we progressed to the curb with our car and driver waiting to go, we were inundated with flashbulbs going off everywhere. As Tom opened the rear door of the car for me, a photographer stuck his camera into my face, and the flash went off. Then, Tom turned to the photographer and with a quick jab to the chin the guy was flattened and lying on the ground. Tom quickly jumped into the back seat with me, and the driver took off, hoping we could outrun the phalanx of journalists. It was crazy! I was so embarrassed to think that my husband of only a few minutes could be so crazy as to deck a journalist. In this day and age, I can't imagine the lawsuits that would follow.

The wedding reception was held at Riverside Golf Club. There was great food, and the booze flowed freely, all paid for by my father. I had such a great time I hated to leave, but it was time to go.

We left by car for Fort Lauderdale, where Tom's cousins lived. It was a three-day trip from Chicago, with overnight stops in Chattanooga and Atlanta, sight seeing at historic sites along the way.

We arrived in Ft. Lauderdale on November 19, where Tom's cousins owned beachside cottages. We were lucky enough to stay in one of those cottages. However, that November was the coldest ever. Houses and cars had no heaters, except some houses had small space heaters built into a wall. I turned on the stove and all the burners to get some heat in our cottage. His cousin's car had no heat either when we went someplace. That's how automakers shipped cars to Florida, probably figuring they didn't need heat. I don't remember it snowing, but it was cold enough.

One day we decided to go for a walk. It was November 27, barely a week after we arrived in Ft. Lauderdale. We no sooner entered the street than photographers were there, taking our pictures. I was perturbed. Turned out that Jean, Tom's cousin, had notified the local newspaper, the Miami Herald. Mel Kenyon is the photographer whose name is on the photo, copyright Miami Herald. We couldn't get away from publicity.

The picture I planned to put here was taken by *Mel Kenyon of the Miami Herald*

It shows Tom and I walking the streets of Ft. Lauderdale near the beach where our cottage was. It was one week after we arrived in Ft. Lauderdale. McClatchy wanted several hundred dollars to allow me to print the photo.

We did have fun enough, however. Ft. Lauderdale is a different climate with lots of different things to do. We went to the horse races and had great fun. Tom's cousin, Jean, knew how to use the dope sheets to figure out good bets. I just picked whatever horse looked good, occasionally looking at the dope sheets, and particularly liked betting on long shots to win, place or show. I made a bit of money. We were there for two weeks, long enough for the weather to warm up and enjoy the ocean and sand.

We went many places in Florida – the Everglades, Key West, Ocala, Winter Haven, Orlando, Cypress Gardens, the Everglades and places on the Gulf Coast. We had great fun in Miami Beach, where Dr. and Mrs. Moser were staying in a beachfront high-rise. We went to dinner with them. It was a real treat.

On the drive back to Chicago we stayed in Gainesville, Georgia, and Knoxville, Tennessee. We drove through the Smoky Mountains. What scenery. We also stopped in many historic places. I found the Cherokee Nation history to be fascinating and heartbreaking.

On arriving home, I discovered my boss had fired me for showing up two days late. I tried to explain the huge snowstorms and the accumulation of snow through Georgia, Tennessee and Kentucky, but he was having none of it.

Right after we married, Tom and I received an invitation (or multiple invitations for various events) for Uncle Ike's second inauguration in January 1957. Tom fully expected that Dad and Mother would pay for our trip.

Dad said, "No way, you are married now, you can pay your own way!"

Fame didn't go far in our family! The Eisenhower magic only works with outsiders!

After I had returned home from our honeymoon, I had to make an inventory of every gift I received. It was considered only proper that thank you notes be written to every single gift-giver. I wrote thank you notes day after day, meticulously, but it was tiresome slogging. However, I did appreciate the gifts. I did get it done, spending many days to do so.

We received a special telegram from Uncle Ike and Aunt Mamie, and a special gift from them – a sterling silver wedding ring ashtray with the following inscription:

"Kathryn and Elbridge Morgan
From
The President and Mrs. Eisenhower"

Yes, Tom's real name was Elbridge Sawyer Morgan, named for his mother's father, Elbridge Sawyer. He was called "Tom Sawyer" all his life, consequently, the nickname "Tom."

It was a good thing that Tom had accepted a job with Butler Manufacturing Company and was due to report for duty in Kansas City in January. His brother, Bill, who lived in Prairie Village, Kansas, outside of Kansas City had arranged the interview for Tom. Bill was a good friend of someone who worked for Butler. What are friends for? It got us a good job in Kansas City.

Bill, and his wife, Woody, were expecting their first child. We had a lot of good times with them. There were other couples we got to know. Most of them lived in Kansas City suburbs southwest of the city in Kansas.

Kansas was a dry state, and Missouri, where we lived in Country Club Plaza, was not dry. The state liquor store was down the street, not far from where we lived. Anytime we were going to visit friends in Kansas (Prairie Village or other places) our friends would give us a list of booze they wished us to purchase for them. We would go to the liquor store and get what they all wanted, stash it in the trunk of our car, and then go back to our apartment and wait for a time. The Kansas State Patrol would sit just across the state line near the liquor store, waiting for people to come out of the liquor store and head for Kansas. They got nabbed every time. Fortunately, we never did, but we took circuitous routes to evade where those cops were waiting.

While living in Kansas City, we attended the Presbyterian Church there, where I was baptized at the age of 23. By this age, my church going was eclectic: raised in the Methodist church since I was a child until graduation from high school, married in a Congregational Church, and now baptized a Presbyterian. Further future forays would take me to a Methodist church in Roscoe, Illinois, to a Presbyterian Church in Tucson, and to Presbyterian churches in Apache Junction and Mesa, Arizona. Then, later to an ELCA Lutheran Church in Fountain Hills, Arizona, and Mesa,

Arizona, back to my old Presbyterian Church in Mesa where I stayed for several years before moving to California. I'm now a Presbyterian for good. But, I digress.

Uncle Arthur
Kansas City 1957-1959

Uncle Arthur (Arthur Bradford Eisenhower) was my oldest uncle, the oldest of the Eisenhower brothers. He was born in 1886 in Hope, Kansas, a little more than a year after my grandparents married. Arthur was barely 18 when he left home about 1904 after graduating from high school. He went to Kansas City where jobs were more plentiful than in Abilene or anyplace else in the area. He got a job in a bank doing janitorial work and worked his way up over the years to become Vice President of the Bank and President of the Kansas City Board of Trade. He worked very hard all his life and his hard work paid off. He was the only Eisenhower brother who never went to college and regretted that fact all his life.

In fact, Arthur was one of the founders of the Kansas City Board of Trade. It was founded to provide farmers in the area a secure and reliable way to sell their produce at reasonable prices.

When he first went to Kansas City, he married a girl named Alida. Dad (Earl) and his brother Ed went to Kansas City to visit Arthur and discovered him in the process of buying a gun. Inquiring as to why he would be buying a gun (who was never a hunter), Arthur said he was planning on killing his wife, as he found her in bed with another man. Fortunately, Earl and Ed managed to stop him and put an end to his murderous scheme, or the Eisenhowers would have had a black sheep in their family. For sure! I've often wondered how Uncle Ike's run for the presidency would have turned out if he had a brother who was a murderer. History might have turned out differently!

Eventually, Arthur allowed Alida to obtain a divorce, being the ultimate gentleman that he was. Unfortunately, she and her lawyer took Arthur for just about every dime he earned for the rest of his life. It's a long and ugly story. I had the files related to Arthur's divorce locked in the Eisenhower Library. The files will not be revealed for another half century.

Arthur later met Louise Grieb, a wealthy widow, fell in love with her and they married shortly after that. Louise had a daughter Katherine by her first husband. Arthur adopted Katherine.

About the time Uncle Ike was elected president, he decided to have family trees made up, one for each of his brothers. This genealogy showed the ancestors of David and Ida Eisenhower and data of the six Eisenhower Brothers and their wives and children around a centered picture of David and Ida on their wedding day.

This family tree listed Katherine as an "adopted daughter" of Arthur. Louise, Arthur's wife, hit the ceiling and demanded that the first family trees or genealogies be trashed. She insisted new ones be made showing Katherine as the "daughter" of Arthur, with the "adopted" designation removed. Fortunately, the original six copies still existed – they were never destroyed – so each family then ended up with two copies of the genealogy family tree. All of Louise's fuss didn't accomplish anything.

Tom and I lived in Kansas City from about January 1957 to April 1959. When we were living there, we had the opportunity to socialize with Uncle Arthur and Aunt Louise. Louise was a very sociable person, on the surface very nice and polite, but underneath a very publicity-driven person. Arthur was a quiet man who didn't say a whole lot. Louise seemed to do most of the talking. They took us to dinner a couple of times – once at the Kansas City Club and another time to the Kansas City Country Club.

Sometime in 1957 Uncle Arthur had a bad heart attack; the following January (1958) he died at the age of 71.

Following Arthur's death, while funeral plans were still being decided, Louise called me at work one day. I was working for Ben Hargis, Vice President for Sales for Commander-Larrabee Milling Company, a division of Archer-Daniels-Midland. Louise said she wanted me to come stay with her since she was now alone in her big house. I tried to explain that I could not get the time off work as I had not worked at Commander-Larrabee long enough. She kept pestering me. My responses to her she was not accepting.

Finally, I called Mother and told her what was happening. I asked her, "Should I stay with Louise, no matter what?"

Mother emphatically stated, "No, you should not be staying with Louise. She has friends living nearby who can stay with her."

Louise was furious. She immediately went next door to Mr. Butler's house. Mr. Butler was my husband, Tom's, boss. She complained that I was rude to her. The next day when Tom went to work, he got a dressing-down because of "my attitude." Tom was furious. He felt I should go stay with Louise. My job would have been in jeopardy if I took time off. I didn't want that to happen. Besides that, Mother told me I shouldn't have to stay with Louise. End of story.

Louise was a publicity freak. I always felt that she wanted the publicity more than she wanted me with her. She had a habit of calling the Press every time she went someplace, stating to them, something like, "I'm going to the Kansas City Country Club today. I'll be there at a certain time if you would like to get some pictures."

When a close relative of the president dies, and the president's attendance at the funeral is a must, the protocol is mind-bending for other people. I had gotten used to White House protocol, so I knew what to do, or whom I should follow or talk with if I had any questions. However, Louise had another mind about the matter. She had stated several times in the past, dating back to Dwight's first inauguration, that she was the one deserving of the most deference in the family since she married to the oldest Eisenhower brother. In other words, President or not, she was the head honcho, ahead of President Eisenhower. This attitude created a three-ring circus every time the family gathered.

For Arthur's funeral, the plan was that the entire Eisenhower family – all his brothers and their families – would meet at Arthur and Louise's mansion in Mission Hills, Kansas, outside of

Kansas City. We would then motor to the cemetery where the service would take place. We all gathered at Arthur and Louise's home and waited for the President to show up. By all protocol, the President is always the last person to enter a room and the first person to leave. He flew in Air Force One (named the Columbine) to an Army base nearby, then by helicopter to Olathe, from there by limousine to Arthur and Louise's home where we were all waiting.

Uncle Ike entered the grand living room with his Secret Service escorts. We all waited for Louise to make her entrance. Half and hour went by, and no Louise. No one knew what was going on.

Finally, an exasperated President Eisenhower stated that he would go upstairs and find out what was going on. His Secret Service entourage followed him upstairs, who all accosted Louise and asked as politely as possible, something like: "What in the world is going on?" (The Language was much stronger than that!) Uncle Ike was furious!

Louise refused to budge, flatly stating that she, as the widow of the oldest Eisenhower brother, was the highest-ranking member of the clan. She unequivocally stated that she would be the last one to descend the steps into the living room where the rest of us waited.

The Secret Service agents tried and tried to talk to her and explain Presidential protocol. She would have none of it and refused to go downstairs.

Finally, Uncle Ike, thoroughly disgusted by this time stated, "Oh, I'll go down, and she can follow me!" In a voice that indicated that he was thoroughly disgusted.

Only then would Louise finally make her grand entrance, regally descending the stairs to her waiting subjects.

Not long after Arthur's funeral, Louise decided to pull up stakes and move to a Park Avenue apartment in New York City. In the process, she had Arthur's casket dug up and moved to a cemetery in New York City. After a couple years of loneliness, she decided to move back to Mission Hills. Louise had Arthur's casket dug up a second time and re-buried for the final time.

Louise died alone and forgotten at her home in Mission Hills in September 1979, age 87. It took three days to discover her body. Aunt Mamie followed her in death in November 1979, age 82. The two hated each other. I've always wondered what their meeting again might be like!

But, Tom and I did enjoy getting to know Uncle Arthur. He was a quiet-spoken person and a joy to be around.

Houston, Texas
1959 to 1962

We stayed another year in Kansas City; then Butler Manufacturing Company transferred us to Houston, where Tom would become one of their salesmen working out of their main office.

We rented a cute little two-bedroom house in West University Place, across the street from Weingarten's. West University Place was a tiny town about one square mile, totally surrounded by the giant city of Houston, which was spreading out in all directions, even then.

Living in Texas was a culture change, perhaps even at times a "culture shock." I loved Texans and will never forget the friends we had there.

One of our neighbors, Jim Vrba, came running down to our house one day to warn us of "a Blue Norther on the way!"

I asked, "What in the world is a Blue Norther?"

He explained that's when the temperature drops (so many) degrees and the wind comes from the north.

Wow! These people didn't know the meaning of blue northers. After living in Pennsylvania, Ohio and Chicago, Illinois, blue northers didn't bother us. We didn't relate well to his warning.

But we loved Jim and his wife, Pearl and their two girls, Kathy and Johanna, who babysat our two little girls occasionally. The other neighbors next door were Katherine and Tom Massengale. They were a godsend to me at times, too. Katherine would take my two baby girls for an hour every day so I could get a nap. What a blessing!

However, we did heed a hurricane warning when Hurricane Carla came pounding across the Gulf Coast in September 1961. Carla was the first Category 5 hurricane of the 1961 season. It hit numerous towns along the Texas Gulf Coast, and much of the windfall reached us about 50 miles inland. The hurricane peeled roof shingles and tarpaper from our roof. The landlord had to get workmen out there the next day so no further damage would happen.

People in our neighborhood boarded up windows. Neither Tom nor I had any sense about what to do, so we did not board up our windows. However, except for the roof, we had no damage.

Our daughter, Karla, was almost a year old at the time. People often asked us if she were named for the hurricane. I always had to reply, "No, the hurricane was named after her!"

Texas was wonderful – people lived outside – barbecues were the every weekend thing, and these people knew how to grill. Especially Jim Vrba – his smoked sausages were famous. Every time we grilled, Jim would have to produce his famous sausages.

We had to get used to the weather in Houston. The air was so hot, muggy and sticky I swore I'd never be dry again. Our little house had no air conditioning, either. When we first moved there in April of 1959, I was five months pregnant with Tracy, which meant I had to endure most of the summer until she was born in August. I thought I would die, so hot and miserable it was. Bedding would be soaking wet in the morning. Our landlord finally agreed to let us put a window air conditioner in one window, which cooled our bedroom and the den. Soon after, we added a second window unit, enabling us then to cool the whole house. What a blessed relief. I do not recommend Houston unless you have air conditioning!

Summers were interesting – it would be bright and sunny in the mornings, but by noon the sky would cloud up, and the rains would come. I soon learned to get my laundry hung out early to beat the noon rain.

Another element of living in Houston was the preponderance of bugs, snakes, and other critters. One time, we entered the house and saw a snake slithering around the corner. Not knowing where it went, we immediately sealed off the bedroom and looked around thoroughly, inspecting every nook and cranny, and determined the snake was not in our bedroom. The next day we found the snake wrapped around the tube in the TV set, fried. Apparently we had watched TV, not knowing the snake was there.

Cockroaches were ubiquitous. Everyone had them – even the best homes in River Oaks. We attended a very posh event in River Oaks, and while the butlers were passing around drinks and food, cockroaches were scurrying about the room. You just couldn't get rid of them. Shortly after moving to Houston, I opened the potato bin in the kitchen to find hundreds of cockroaches swarming all over the place. Yuck! Ugly! What a chore! Had to call an exterminator to get rid of them, but it was a never-ending job. One day, my nine-month-old Tracy was crawling along the floor, and as I was watching her, a cockroach came out of nowhere and she grabbed it and ate it. Oh, more yuck! I called the doctor, and he said not to worry, that everything would come out in the end!!! She giggled for the rest of the day.

I had to very careful gardening, pulling weeds and such. Always be on the lookout for snakes. We had little snakes that looked like coral snakes, so gardening was a dicey activity.

While we were living in Houston, Uncle Ike came to town in October 1960. He was scheduled to speak at Rice University. He and his entourage stayed at the Shamrock Hilton on the 14th floor. (In later years when Tom and I and our girls came back to Houston for a company conference, the company put us up at the Shamrock Hilton in the same suite that Uncle Ike had. However, we were then expected to be the party suite – our girls loved it!)

Mother and I got to visit Uncle Ike at the Shamrock Hilton. Mother had come to stay with me for a couple weeks after Karla's birth. Dad was not scheduled to come for another week or so; consequently he was not with us at the time.

While we were talking with Uncle Ike, he asked us if he should endorse Nixon, who was running for President at the time. Apparently Uncle Ike was fence-sitting this issue. Eventually, almost belatedly, he did give Nixon a tepid endorsement but was none too thrilled about the issue. For some reason or other, which we never discussed, Uncle Ike was becoming disenchanted with Nixon.

I remember also Uncle Ike talking about Senator McCarthy. He despised McCarthy and his tactics and had tried to ignore him for the most part. However, McCarthy was not to be ignored!

Tom was so excited to be part of the Eisenhower entourage; he told his bosses at Butler Manufacturing that he could get them tickets for Uncle Ike's speech at Rice University. He came home and gave me the news. I was a bit perturbed that he promised something that he might not be able to deliver. The speech would be the next night, and there was not much time left. I called the publicity staff (all fellows I knew) and asked them if a couple additional tickets might be available for Uncle Ike's speech. They informed me that no more tickets were available under any circumstance. When the President appears anywhere, attendance is strictly controlled, and we have to live with that. If I had known a week prior, tickets "might" have been available.

Tom had to return to work and sheepishly admit that he could not obtain tickets for his bosses. His name apparently became mud. After that he got crosswise with some bosses in that office. He then quit Butler and went to work for National Steel, also selling steel buildings.

Tom had to go to Washington, D.C. on a business trip. I believe it was about 1960 or 1961, but am not positive. I managed to get him an audience with Uncle Ike in the Oval Office. When Tom showed up at the White House, I guess he must have outdone himself. For, years later, in talking with Uncle Milton he told me that Uncle Ike had said something like, "I don't ever want to see that man again!" (The word used to describe Tom was pretty graphic!) So much for good impressions! Uncle Ike had some not so kind words to say about my husband.

Cincinnati (Madeira, Ohio)
1962 to 1966

National Steel transferred Tom to the Cincinnati office in the spring of 1962. We found a cute little brick bungalow, three bedrooms, one bath, kitchen, dining room and living room with a full basement. It was in Madeira, a few miles east of Cincinnati. It was the first house we ever bought, and it cost $16,000. That's less than what we pay for a car nowadays. When we sold it a few years later to a local fireman, we got $16,000.

The big problem doing laundry was that the washing machine and dryer were in the basement. Lugging dirty laundry downstairs was a chore, especially since I was now pregnant with Tommy, my third child. One day I was carrying a load downstairs and about nine months pregnant when I tripped and fell the entire flight to the bottom where I landed on top of the laundry. No worse for the wear; no bruises or broken bones, I proceeded with the laundry and everything was OK.

I met several neighbors when we first moved in. A neighbor told me that she had done the school census recently. They counted 400 school-age kids in our neighborhood (that's two parallel streets each about a block and a half long), with the school itself about a block away. I was stunned and couldn't believe such a number.

However, when Halloween showed up, and kids started knocking at our door, it was a nightmare. Tom was traveling, as usual, and my two girls were two and three years old. I had just started feeding them when the doorbell started ringing. I had made popcorn balls and quickly ran out, then resorted to some cookies and candy I had available. Then I ran out of stuff to hand out. I was warned about the number of kids in the neighborhood, but just couldn't comprehend such a number. I finally had to turn out the porch light and hope they would go away. I told Tom that next year HE WOULD be home for Halloween.

Our two boys – Tommy and Michael – were born in January 1963 and September 1965, respectively. Tommy's birth was a nightmare. My regular doctor was out of town, leaving me with a substitute doctor. Husband Tom was in Detroit for a meeting. The worst snowstorm of the season was descending on Cincinnati, and on top of that burglars attempted to get into my house.

The bad guys rapped on my back door about 8 PM. Seeing three guys with apparently bad attitudes, I quickly slammed the door and locked it, then immediately called the police. Police came shortly and after asking me some questions said those bad guys were guilty of robbing a local store and wanted to know what their car looked like and what direction they went. I'm assuming the Police caught the crooks. But the episode left me in a state of nerves and my labor started – two weeks early.

I called the doctor, and he pooh-poohed the idea, said I wasn't due for two weeks, and to lie down, and the labor would stop. He didn't pick up on the fact that my first two pregnancies were also two weeks early! O my gosh! I also had a tub of ironing to do. I didn't want my girls dressed in wrinkled clothes while I was gone. New mothers generally stayed in the hospital for a week or so. Nothing worked. Labor continued. I called the doctor back, then I called Tom in Detroit, then I called my next-door neighbor to take me to the hospital.

When I got to the hospital in Mariemont (pronounced like it was spelled "mary-mont"), it was jammed with people – this was January 9, 1963. Emergency Room was packed, and there were people on gurneys in all the hallways. Must have been a phase of the moon or something!

Medical personnel placed me on a gurney in a hallway near the delivery room, and I just lay there as nurses and hospital personnel streamed by me. I finally had to scream at a nurse running by and convince her the baby was on its way. She took one look, screamed for attendants and quickly hauled me into the delivery room. Nurses and attendants delivered Tommy just after midnight on January 10, 1963, just as the doctor came running into the room pulling on his surgical gloves. I was kind of put out when I got the doctor's bill.

Husband Tom arrived shortly after that, his plane having arrived from Detroit and was the last plane to land at Cincinnati airport before they closed it down due to the snowstorm.

When Michael was born in September 1965, the doctor told the nursing staff that I delivered quickly, so keep an eye on me. Oh, they did all right. They stuck me on a gurney with my feet in stirrups and all my glory available to see through the windows so the nurses "could keep an eye on me." Everyone walking down the hallway could also see, including the paperboy delivering the early morning edition of the newspaper. I'm glad I could hide my face.

Michael was born with epilepsy, wall-eyes, and malformed facial features and severe dental problems due to the small jaw size. It would take years of surgeries to make his face look normal. We had to keep him on Phenobarbital to control the seizures. He would often have seizures and would be unconscious for hours. Doctors originally diagnosed him as "retarded." However, I wanted further evaluation. After a week of tests, keeping Michael in the hospital for five days, the doctors declared him to be "borderline" retarded.

There is not much to say about Madeira or Cincinnati, except it seems you had to live there a hundred years to be accepted. I went to church with a neighbor one Sunday. The church that day featured several groups, including women's circles, which I thought I might like to join.

My friend told me that wouldn't be possible because "you have to be invited to join." I never went back to that church or any other church in the area while we lived there.

We had some very dear friends – Tony and Dodi – who had moved to the Cincinnati area about the same time we did. We had met them earlier as they were related to friends of my parents who also lived in La Grange. What a great couple! Lots of fun, four little kids the same ages as our kids. We got along well.

One day Dodi said to me, "How do you make friends in this town?"

Dodi was the friendliest person I've ever known, an absolute angel. I figured the lack of friends in Cincinnati wasn't my fault or Dodi's.

One of the problems living in a neighborhood with so many children was the constant round of all the common childhood diseases – colds, flu, measles, chicken pox, mumps, you name it. I was constantly picking up the kids' illnesses and ended up with strep throats, bronchial congestion, pneumonia, and colds. I had all the common childhood illnesses except mumps, but fortunately didn't get mumps, though I felt like it with painful lumps in my throat, but, fortunately, no fever. Michael was the only one who never got anything. Makes me wonder about his immune system.

The good thing about working out of the Cincinnati office was that Tom's territory included Kentucky. I often made trips around Kentucky with him, visiting various state historic sites. We made friends with a couple near Frankfurt, had some great times with them. Salty Dogs were the order of the day when we visited them.

Tom had quite a few buddies in National Steel's office with whom he worked, and we would often get together with other couples. One day in November of 1963, we all went to Dayton to celebrate two birthdays – Tom's and another friend – who shared the November 22 birthdate.

When we got to Dayton, we learned the news of President Kennedy's assassination. Instead of celebrating birthdays, the eight of us spent the day in front of the TV. Sitting in front of the TV was not the celebration for which we came to Dayton.

However, during this planned get-together, we all were sitting around talking, and someone mentioned "Tom's girlfriend in Louisville." Seemed like everybody but me knew of Tom's affairs. The room got deadly silent as everyone then looked at me. I didn't feel anything – I was just numb.

I do not know what happened between National Steel and Tom. In early 1966, he quit National Steel and took a job with Bob Proctor in Rockford, Illinois, in direct sales of steel buildings. Bob had a metal building dealership.

Rockford/Roscoe, Illinois
1966 to 1971

We moved to Roscoe, Illinois in April 1966. Michael was seven months old. The others were three, five and six. The only place Tom could find to rent was a two-story newly built house just off Burr Oak Road about a mile or so east of Roscoe. I loved it there. Tom couldn't have found a better place. He was so afraid I wouldn't like it.

We joined the Methodist Church – one of the only two churches in town (the other was Congregational) when we moved to Roscoe. Wonderful group of people. I was a piano player, and consequently put my skills to use directing the children's choir. One of the things I noticed about children's choirs was that they sang beautifully during practice in the basement, but when they had to sing in the sanctuary they acted like a bunch of scared mice.

I determined to overcome this problem with the children. We would practice our songs in the basement fellowship hall as usual. A couple weeks before we were due to sing, I would take the kids up to the sanctuary, put them in the choir loft and turn on the organ. Now, I am NOT and never have been an organ player. My gift was as a piano player. However, the keyboard structure of the organ is similar. I would turn on the organ, find the right sound, and play the melody the kids would sing. That got them used to singing with the organ, which is what they would have to do on the Sunday they were scheduled to sing.

They would be hesitant at first, but the more I worked with them, the better they got. Then I would have them sing the songs a cappella while I stood in the back of the church to listen. I would constantly pressure them to sing louder so I could hear them. They had to know that people in the back of the church wanted to hear them also. It worked. We had the best children's choir ever.

My organ-playing career was just getting started.

After children's choir practice one Thursday, I had just arrived home when the phone rang. It was the church secretary asking if I could play the organ for Sunday service.

I replied, "Heavens, no, I'm not an organ player."

She explained that Mrs. Shugars, the church organist, had fallen on an icy sidewalk and was in the hospital with a broken hip. They were looking for a substitute organ player. The secretary said she heard me during choir practice, and I certainly was an organ player.

I said "no" again. Conversation ended.

A few minutes later, at home, I got a call from Mrs. Shugars from her hospital bed. She was very stern, very strict.

She told me, "Get out a pad and pencil, and I will tell you how to play the organ!"

Wow! Really? OK. I found a pad and pencil and with that propped up next to me, and with the phone in one hand and pencil in the other, I prepared to listen. With Mrs. Shugars you listened!

She explained to me how the organ stops worked and which ones to pull for certain hymns. I told her I had no training in working the foot pedal, which was beyond me at that time. She told me not to worry about the foot pedal, just to pull out a certain stop, and that would compensate.

Story continued – I became an organ player. Another lady, Anne Hardy, my friend, had an organ at home, so she was familiar with organ ministration. We both agreed to alternate Sundays to keep the music flowing during Mrs. Shugars' absence. Both of us had to practice on the church organ during the week.

Then, the worst happened. The roof of our sanctuary was a structure that resembled an umbrella. Repairs were not done for many years due to lack of funds. Many of the "slats" or struts of the umbrella were no longer "hooked up" to the main strut. If you looked closely, you could see that.

The preacher at the time knew the roof was dangerous, so he called in the county building inspector, who promptly condemned the building. Our services then had to be conducted in the basement until workmen repaired the roof. We could not get a new roof until the congregation ponied up enough to cover repairs. Tom and I gave a considerable sum of money, as I'm sure others did too. Repairs finally got done after several months.

While a member of this church, we had two different ministers. One was an experienced parson who had worked several church venues over the years. The other was a newly graduated pastor. Both became friends of mine and would come to visit. The older pastor came when there was a new snowfall. He just wanted to enjoy the beauty of the countryside with the new fallen snow. He also would visit us on weekends and sometimes bring his bottle of whatever he had. One weekend he brought some Greek Metaxa, which we finished by the end of the evening. Once, he said, after finishing the Metaxa, "Oops, I have a wedding to participate in tonight!" I hope the Metaxa got him through the ceremony. The other pastor, who came after him, would drop by at odd times. He only liked to enjoy the countryside where we lived. He was earnest but struggling to keep up with the older congregation. His wife was out of favor with the congregation. She worked full time and insisted she would *not* be an associate pastor!

One day in the early summer of 1966, while living in Roscoe, Illinois, at the age of about eight months Michael was crawling across the yard. We were all sitting in the yard enjoying the sunset after dinner. Our puppy was happily gnawing on a big bone. I wasn't watching closely enough when Michael made a grab for the puppy's bone and the puppy promptly attacked him, tearing up his eyelid and tear duct. I called the doctor while holding Michael in my arms, and the doctor told me to go to a hospital in Rockford. Tom stayed home with the other kids as I rushed Michael to the hospital, with him bleeding profusely from the wound. During the surgery, doctors told me that his "wall eyes" should be corrected with surgery. Then, he had to endure four more surgeries to correct the wall-eyed muscular imbalance. That ended up being the fifth surgery on his eyes. Then doctors fitted him with special glasses and we had to tape them to his head. Have you ever seen a baby crawling around with pop-bottle glasses?

Our landlord had built the house on land adjacent to his mother and stepfather's property. Alice and Wilbur were their names and I loved those two people. Alice taught me much about cooking, canning and preparing many good sauces. Wilbur was full of stories and sage advice. He supplied me with manure for my garden from his sheep farm. It was the best fertilizer in the world!

I loved living here – lots of space for kids to roam, a garden for me to grow vegetables of all kinds. For several weeks in late summer we had fresh corn on the cob for dinner. We were near the Jolly Green Giant farms, and it was fascinating to watch how that company managed the produce they harvested. Late at night, several combines would come up the road past our house and turn into the first Jolly Green Giant land. The combines lined up, side-by-side and one or two runs across the field and back and they were done with this field, then on to the next field, where the same scenario took place. Harvest was done in a few hours for acres of land.

Our home was not far from Lake Geneva where we would occasionally go for dinner. It was about an hour drive east of us. It was a beautiful place, and I always enjoyed going there for dinner.

Living about a mile east of Roscoe, out old Burr Oak Road, was wonderful. We had no traffic except tractors, lots of creeks, bugs to catch, snakes to avoid, places to hang swings, places to dig forts, and who knows what else. There were lots of places to sled ride in the winter also since cows were in the barn during the winter. One meadow had an ancient child's playhouse built near a creek that ran through the property. The granddaughter of the owner of the property never went down into that meadow. My kids thought that playhouse was something special. My children always remembered this place as their most favorite place.

My children made friends living here who have been their friends all these years. Roscoe was special – I still remember friends from that time – Jeannie, Anne, Martha. God Bless you all!

Dad and Mom's visit summer 1966

A few months after we moved to Roscoe, Dad and Mom came to visit. They spent several days.

Dad loved it. He always liked country living and big gardens.

Dad and Mom were planning on moving to Scottsdale in a few months. At the time, they were going to visit all their friends, knowing they would never be back this way again. From La Grange Park, Illinois, they drove to visit us for several days, and then drove on to Pennsylvania to visit the many friends they had there.

One evening after dinner, we were all sitting in the living room talking, watching TV or whatever. We had some drinks after dinner. About 8 o'clock or so, Mother announced she was tired and would go to bed. She made it up the stairs and shortly after that we heard this big thump/crash. I looked baffled.

Dad looked at me and said, "She's your care now."

I did not know what he meant. I rushed upstairs and found my mother in a heap on the floor totally incoherent. I was dumbfounded. She had no idea where she was or what she was doing. I got her undressed, into her nightgown and put her into bed.

The next day Dad had a long talk with me. He told me that doctors had told him he did not have long to live. He told me that and then told me that only one other person, his best friend, knew of his condition. He didn't dare tell Mother. That was the reason they were visiting all their old friends, driving as far as Pennsylvania to their old neighborhood, so Mother could see all her friends before moving to Scottsdale. He realized that once they moved to Arizona they would probably never see their friends again. Dad had a very bad heart. At this time he was actually beginning to see double.

He told me a lot of things: – how Mother never wanted me – she wanted a red-headed boy, and I was neither red-headed nor a boy. He told me how she would ignore me and only handle me when necessary. That explains a lot of why she treated me as she did when I was a kid. He then went on to tell me that the reason he took me many places with him and tried to be with me was to compensate for Mother's lack of affection and care. He was a stoic old German, certainly not the huggy-kissy type at all. But he did care.

After this conversation, I realized how much he had loved me. He also explained that Mother was an alcoholic. He had spent a lot of time over the years caring for her. Now, it was my turn. However, they were moving to Scottsdale because my Brother was living there, and Bud had said that he would never leave Scottsdale. Whereas, my husband was always finding a job somewhere else, and we kept moving. No one knew where we would land next. Dad did not think it a good idea to locate Mother anywhere near me, not knowing where we might move next. She and I never got along that well, but she doted on Bud. Moving to Scottsdale was the best solution for Mother.

I also learned some years later, that she had started drinking in high school. During Prohibition, people would find booze, call their friends, and arrange "drinking parties." Mother would stand up her dates in order to attend a "drinking party." Her best friend from childhood days also told me she had been in a nursing or care home when she was in high school. No one ever knew details. This information came to me later in life from correspondence mother had saved and from her friend mentioned above.

It was February 1967 when they moved to Scottsdale, where they stayed with Bud, my brother until they found a place they could buy. They found a cute little three-bedroom slump-block bungalow right on Indian School Road for only $16,000, as much as we had spent on our first home in Madeira, Ohio in 1962. The house on Indian School Road was demolished probably around 1990 to widen Indian School Road.

Many happy hours were spent here with Bud and his girlfriend, Judy, who later became his wife; plus our family of six and many of my parents' friends. We would visit in the future in 1967, 1968, and 1969.

Roscoe House
1966 - 1971

We spent the winter of 1966-67 in our nice rented two-story house in Roscoe until the owner told us to move as he wanted his house back in the spring of 1967. Now! We just informed him we couldn't move that quickly as we were now a family of six people and needed to find a place.

What we found was a lot that we bought from a local farmer. He subdivided his land, and we got an acre on Lovesee Road at the corner of what is now Harnish Road. We built a house in three months, acting as our own contractor. Tom knew lots of sub-contractors, and we did most of the finishing inside – floors, walls, etc. It was a hurry job.

I loved this house – long, low, ranch style, stained dark brown rough-out cedar with white and black trim on the windows. It had a picture window on the white stone front overlooking the canyon across the road. The house was 3,000 square feet with mudroom and laundry, family room, an oversized garage that fit two cars and a tractor and a huge freezer, three good-sized bedrooms, and two full bathrooms. I had "stretched" the blueprint floor plan to add a mudroom and additional space to the garage for our tractor and freezer.

I designed the house to fit the tree-filled lot, starting with some standard blueprints. The kitchen cabinets between the kitchen and eating area were double-faced, and I designed everything for maximum efficiency. The double-faced cabinets were between the kitchen and dining areas. My only mistake was in using the portable dishwasher that we already had instead of having one built in. I designed the girls' bedroom with a huge bay window with seating and storage under the window. (The bay window is gone now, replaced by regular window after a storm demolished a corner of the house.) The girls loved playing in that room as the storage area not only was a good place for toys, but also used to play hide-and-seek.

We had two septic systems put in – one for regular use and the other for laundry waste. The well was very deep – we went down so far we struck an underground river. The well had a

50-gallon reserve tank so when the power went out we still had drinking water. The gas appliances also came in handy when the power was out, as did our huge over-sized freezer in the garage. We never had big problems with power outages. We just waited power to come back on and in the meantime it was like camping.

One of the blessings of living in rural Roscoe was the 4-H organization. All the kids I knew were involved, including ours. I became a sewing teacher and cooking teacher. 4-H has very specific rules for sewing and cooking. The meatloaf they were required to prepare was a "depression era" recipe, which consisted of half meat and half oatmeal. It was truly ugly! Sewing instructions were quite specific about the length of stitches, size of the hem, length of the skirt, etc. It was arduous, but all the little girls accomplished the sewing. I was also a pianist for 4-H for the vocal competition. We took second place in a county-wide competition. The kids sang and danced. We had a great routine put together.

Our kids got involved with 4-H here in Roscoe, Winnebago County, when they were very young. Consequently, I was also involved. I taught cooking and sewing. The 4-H method was very strict. There were precise guidelines to follow for sewing the skirt the girls had to make. And, very strict recipe instructions for the dinner and especially the meatloaf the girls had to prepare. The meatloaf recipe was what we called "depression-era meatloaf." It was half hamburger and half oatmeal, and it was truly awful. But, nevertheless, that was the recipe we had to follow. The girls' final test was to cook and serve a complete meal using the "depression era" recipes. Ugh! But they did it, and both earned their badges.

One bright spot in my 4-H career was when we got to compete with other 4-H groups on a countywide basis with a choral presentation. I directed our choral group of eight to twelve (I forget how many there were). We competed locally and won the chance to compete in a wider state celebration in Joliet. We took second place in this statewide competition. Our group sang their hearts out. They came faithfully to every practice. We had lots of movement and varied changes to standard musical numbers. The rules stated that we had to present two songs, and they had to be different. We had to get permission from the "Up With People" organization to use their *Up With People* song. Our second song was *This Land is Our Land.* I was so proud of those kids. Second place was pretty doggone good considering the kids' ages and the competition we were up against. I wonder if any of them remember. I certainly do.

I also accompanied one girl on a French horn solo. She was great – again, she never missed a practice. I can't say enough about 4-H kids.

A lot of 4-H kids in our farm country showed stock animals – cows, goats, pigs, etc. That was always exciting to see how hard they worked and to see their animals shown at the annual county and state fairs. Forever after I've loved going to state fairs, even when I lived in the Phoenix area where it could get so blooming hot!

Fame found me here in Roscoe – it must have been 1968 or 1969. A local newspaper out of Rockford called and asked if they could interview me. I do not know how they learned that I was Dwight Eisenhower's niece. However, they did come all the way out to Roscoe, interviewed me, took some pictures and the article with pictures was in the newspapers a few days later.

FIRST ARIZONA TRIP
December 1967 to January 1968

As planned, we traveled west with the kids in December 1967, leaving about a week before Christmas. Dad had been badgering us for a year, telling us that December is the best time to visit Phoenix. It certainly did live up to his expectations. We had a long drive from Roscoe, Illinois, to Scottsdale, Arizona. I think it took us three days. What I do remember so vividly is the snowstorm we met at Tucumcari, New Mexico. It was snowing so hard that state troopers would not let us go any further west on I-40 until we bought chains for the station wagon. After that, they directed us to Santa Rosa and south, telling us what routes to take to Deming, New Mexico and Interstate 10. Albuquerque was totally snowed in, and nothing was getting through that area at all. We turned south at Santa Rosa and kept going – we didn't dare stop. The snowstorm was behind us the whole way south through New

Mexico, and we knew if we stopped, the storm would engulf us. These south-bound roads were quite a bit narrower than the freeway we had been driving on – only one lane each way and we had to keep moving so as to NOT get stuck. The snow was piling up on these roads, too. It was a very stressful drive.

With a big sigh of relief, we finally made it to Deming where it was raining. I'll take the rain, thank you. At Deming, I called Dad and asked him how we should get to Scottsdale from Deming. His original directions were for us to take I-40 to Flagstaff and go south on Black Canyon Freeway into Phoenix.

Dad's first response was, "What in the world are you doing in Deming?"

"It's a long story, Dad; we'll explain later." We finally got to Scottsdale, a little later than we figured.

While in Scottsdale with my parents, my brother, Bud and his girlfriend (soon to be wife), Judy, took us so many places – Sedona, Oak Creek Canyon, the Verde River, Flagstaff, Prescott, and Montezuma's Castle. They also were our tour directors on trips to Tucson, Tombstone, Kitt Peak Observatory, and the Arizona-Sonora Desert Museum. Then they took us to the Desert Botanical Garden in Phoenix by the Airport and the San Xavier del Bac Mission. This mission is called "The White Dove of the Desert - the old Father Kino mission on the Tohono O'odham, once called the Papago reservation. San Xavier is pronounced by the Papagos as "san-ah-veer," as their language has no sound for "X."

We went to their stomping grounds with their friends, saw some of them get blasted at their local watering holes – and still drive home!!! One guy was so far gone that he drove through every single red light on his way home. He lived a charmed life!

The worst trick was played on me. My brother was bartending at Pinnacle Peak Restaurant in North Scottsdale. A bunch of us went up there for dinner. I sat with my back to the bar, my husband facing me. Bud sent over Margaritas. Boy! Did I go for that drink! I'll have another, thank you. I had no idea how potent Margaritas are, and I must have had several – I lost count, unfortunately. We ate our dinner and afterward, with Bud and Judy and a bunch of friends went up the road to a rustic old, and I mean old cowboy hangout. We would never eat there, but the atmosphere was "different" if you had enough booze in you. Perhaps Greasewood Flats is the place, but it had another name at the time. It was a place where true miners used to hang out. I was so drunk I was dancing with the miners. They told me about it later the next day when I was sober. I NEVER got drunk again! That was a nasty trick on me!

The next day, Dad had planned on driving us to Flagstaff and Oak Creek Canyon and Sedona. I was sooooo hung over. Never before! Never since! The trip was awful for me. I could hardly see, let alone enjoy anything.

Bud and his wife had worked for Senator Goldwater while he was a U.S. Senator. They spent many years in Washington, flying back and forth to their Paradise Valley home on holidays. Consequently, Bud knew Arizona like the back of his hand since he would fly around the state in the Senator's private plane. The Senator never lost a chance to visit his constituents. He knew the Navajos, Hopis, Papagos, and all the other Indian tribes. There were 22 Indian tribes with lands in Arizona and the Senator knew them all personally. My brother did, too, and from him I learned the good arts and crafts of each of the tribes or nations. I got to know which ones made the best jewelry and what kind, who made the best baskets, the best-woven rugs, the best pottery, etc. A lot of Indian ware is made for the tourist trade, and much is made in Japan or China. Buyer beware! Make sure you know stuff before you buy. Know how to recognize the good stuff and deal with reputable dealers. Beware the roadside marketers! I also got to know much of the Indian culture, and in later years would experience that first hand.

Bud personally knew Chief Bear Step, the great grandson of Cochise. Bear Step was a grizzled old man, ancient, but he was still running a small gift shop in Old Town, Scottsdale, where he sold his hand-made turquoise jewelry. Bud and I, with my three oldest children, walked into Bear Step's establishment one day. We bought a few things.

One of the clerks thought Tommy was so cute in his new cowboy hat and outfit with boots and all, said, "Oh, you need this scarf to complete your outfit." The clerk whipped a red scarf off the wall and tied it around Tommy's neck.

Little did he know that Bear Step prized that scarf above all his possessions as it had belonged to his great-grandfather, Cochise! He was furious. Oh, that poor clerk!

A few days later we all walked back into the shop, Tommy sporting his wonderful red scarf, of which he was so proud. As soon as Bear Step saw him, he whipped that scarf off Tommy's neck so fast his head must have spun around. Tommy was given another scarf to compensate.

Bear Step made for Tom and me matching silver and turquoise "Bear Step" rings. They weren't identical, but they were each turquoise bear claws. By the time son Tommy died in 2007, he had both bear step rings, which were buried with him. Tom, my ex-husband, had died in 2000, and Tommy got his Bear Step ring. Once I divorced Tom in 1977, I had given my Bear Step ring to Tommy, which is why he had both rings. He truly treasured those rings because he had met Bear Step personally.

We left Arizona in late January 1968, driving north on Black Canyon Freeway to I-40. Driving through Flagstaff, the snow was piled as high as the rooftops. It's no wonder we couldn't possibly have driven through there in December.

We arrived home in the middle of winter, January 1968. What a change, after sunny Arizona. My thought was "How can people live here?" Then I had to stop and realize, "I live here."

CHRISTMAS 1968
Second Arizona Trip

Dad died December 18, 1968. Calls came in for us to be in Scottsdale a few days later for the funeral/memorial service. I called several airlines and had no luck whatsoever.

Then, Judy, bless her, got on the phone and voila! We had airline reservations to Scottsdale a day or so later. With Judy's connections in the Senate and her knowledge of all the VIPs in Washington and around the country, she got us seats. Just Tom and I came, leaving our kids with friends of ours. I understand a Colonel or General lost his seat on the plane. It does pay to know the right people, and Judy knew them. Being an Eisenhower or a member of the Senator's staff, occasionally has its perks!

We stayed for a couple weeks. Mother was in a very fragile state, but I knew we had to go home. In the meantime, Bud would move in with her. That was a big help. I felt that I wouldn't have to worry about her.

Dad's funeral was well attended. Many prominent people in the area came, including Senator Goldwater, who got out of a sick bed to come. He and Dad had been pretty close. They liked each other and got on well.

After the service, family and friends gathered in Mom's home, and it was like "old home week." Uncle Ed and Uncle Milton were both there. Uncle Ike sent his Aide, Col. Bob Schultz, whom I always liked. Uncle Ike, himself, was bedridden with a bad heart condition and would die about four months later. While we were all sitting around chatting, Bob Schultz mentioned that he was hungry. I immediately jumped up to go to the kitchen for whatever food was available. Bob was ahead of me. He said, "When at a friend's house, we need to feel comfortable and at home!" So, he did make himself at home and at once stuck his head in the fridge to see what was there. Funny guy!

In talking with Uncle Milton, it was like I was talking with my father, so much alike the two were. Uncle Milton had been a surrogate father when I was at Penn State in the early 1950s.

I stayed with Mother for a couple weeks or so. When I left Bud moved in with her. I felt that should accomplish what we needed to do for her.

SPRING 1969
Third Arizona Trip

Dad had always said that we had to see the desert in bloom in the spring. So, we promised him that we would come in April 1969. We flew out, stayed with Mother and Bud moved in with Judy for the duration.

The desert was so utterly beautiful at this time of year; I'm glad we came. The glorious display of desert flowers strewn across the desert was mind-boggling to me. I had never dreamed the desert could bloom so. The evening sunsets were stupendous, it was like God was throwing all those colors across the sky just for me. Bud and Judy showed us many sights that I could never imagine in a harsh desert.

We stayed for three weeks and got to see several sights that we hadn't seen before, went out to eat several times, hitting our favorite restaurants.

Considering everything, mother appeared to be doing all right. Mother seemed to be doing as well as could be expected, but it was all show, as we discovered later.

Tom and I returned home with our four children, and I figured all was well, with Bud living with Mother.

SUMMER 1969
Mother

We (Bud and I) figured Mother needed a change and a chance to get away for a while. We made plane reservations for her, and Bud put her on the plane for Chicago' O'Hare Airport, the closest airport to Roscoe. We were a few minutes late getting to the airport, and I was very concerned, knowing how Mother was terrified of flying. We found her, sitting on her luggage in the baggage claim area, apparently stoned out of her mind. She didn't even know where she was. We got her to the car, but she kept trying to open the car door and get out as we were driving on the freeway. It was a nightmare until we finally got home. Mother was also terrified of riding in a car.

The next day Mother was in better shape, but she was heading for the booze at every chance. I arranged some bridge sessions, knowing how she loved to play bridge, but I had to keep her sober enough to act human and be able to play a decent game of bridge.

She was with me for two or three weeks.

I originally thought this might be a nice break for her, but it was terror for her and a nightmare for me. That poor woman just didn't fit into society anymore.

And, I didn't have the wherewithal to handle her or know what to do. Trying to ration the booze and keep her relatively sober was extremely stressful to me. Playing bridge with friends, mother just wasn't hanging it all together, as we say. Her plight was becoming more and more noticeable.

We finally put her back on a plane to Scottsdale/ Phoenix, but things only got worse from then on.

SCOTTSDALE, CHRISTMAS 1969
Fourth Arizona Trip
Mother

After Dad had died at Christmas 1968 (December 18, 1968), Mother was truly a wreck. She had always been high-strung. The doctor gave her some tranquilizers and told her NOT to drink any booze with the pills.

Consequently, she never took the pills because she had to have her booze. Bud had been living with Mother to make sure she was OK.

Early in December 1969, a year after Dad died, Bud called me, begging me to come to Scottsdale, saying, "I can't handle mom any more. I am going berserk! Please come help me!"

My reply was, "Bud, I can't – I've got a husband, a houseful of kids, and we can't afford to fly to Scottsdale at this time."

Bud replied, "Just come, all of you. I will pay the plane fare for all of you."

Before I made any decisions, I called my friend, Pastor Kempton Hewitt. He had worked with alcoholics at one time. He was a valuable resource. He talked with me for hours on the phone. After talking with him, I had a better understanding of my mother and what I could do to help her.

Our family, all six of us, boarded a plane for Phoenix around Christmas time, 1969, a year after Dad had died.

We got to Mother's house. She had prepared a magnificent meal, being the world's best cook that she was. The table was set, ready to sit down to the meal and Mother was sitting on the arm of the couch drinking a highball. Shortly after that, she announced she was tired and would go to bed.

I told her I'd get her a cup of coffee and bring it to her. We all sat down and ate the dinner she had prepared while she went to bed.

After dinner, I called her doctor. I had his home phone number.

When he answered, and I told him who I was, he asked, "Is she drinking again?"

I replied, "I think the answer might be 'yet,' or 'still'"

The doctor then told me to bring her to his office in downtown Phoenix the next day. He had his office in a high-rise medical office complex in central Phoenix. He told me to use the back street (or alley) entrance, and take an elevator directly to his office. He would make sure no one would be in the office when she came in. God Bless him!

In the meantime, he warned me, do NOT take all the booze away from Mother, but give it to her in small doses, enough to keep her relatively sober. Taking booze away from an alcoholic can produce DTs, which can be very dangerous.

I hid all the bottles I could find, having to scour the house for extraneous bottles of booze. She had been drinking two quarts of rotgut a day for the past year. She was near death and didn't know it. In fact, none of us did. She also wasn't eating enough, either.

The next morning, Mother was madly opening closet and cupboard doors looking for booze. Anything. I felt so sorry for this poor human being who couldn't exist without her fix. I told her I'd fix her a nice warm bath and fix her a drink if she would take a bath. She acquiesced. I got her dressed, gave her another drink and some food and hot coffee. Then we were on the way to the doctor's office.

When we got the doctor's office, he could not have been more reassuring. Slowly he examined Mother, noting all the bruises all over her body (she had fallen many times), that he suggested she sign herself into the hospital. She kept insisting she only had a few bruises, but we knew better.

One of my problems was that if I had to get a commitment order, it would have been a matter of public record. Journalists and reporters scour the court records daily to find out what kind of juicy tidbit they can blow up into a full-blown scandal! She was an Eisenhower! I couldn't do that to her.

The doctor and I talked and talked to Mother. She kept refusing to sign into the hospital. Finally, after about an hour of talking, Mother finally caved and said, "OK, I'll sign the papers."

The doctor and I looked at each other, and both of us breathed a sigh of relief. He knew as well as I did that an Eisenhower being committed to the alcoholic ward of the hospital would be a juicy scandal. So much for being an Eisenhower.

Mother was in the hospital Intensive Care Unit for a week, suffering DTs and close to death. Her liver was solid as a rock and non-functional. I was there, every day, just praying, just sitting, just waiting. At one point, three doctors came to see me, saying that they did not think they could save her, that she was near death.

I replied, "You doctors have done everything you can do, the rest is up to God."

A week later, Mother was finally lucid, but just barely. She stayed in the hospital, in a special recovery unit, for another three weeks. Her room was like a motel room, which she had to keep clean and neat. She also had to report for group therapy sessions twice a day and three times a day report to the dining room for regular meals. The unit was a special psychiatric unit, which was locked and barred to the public. I was not allowed to visit her very often, and then only briefly.

Finally, she got to come home. The healing process was just beginning. While in the hospital the doctors kept asking her, "Mrs. Eisenhower, why are you here?"

Her reply was always, "Because I fell and had so many bruises."

They kept after her, always asking the same question.

Finally, her answer was, "Because I am an alcoholic."

Only then could recuperation begin.

A year later when mother went back for her checkup, the doctor pronounced her "a miracle." I do believe her cure was a miracle! She was 60 at the time.

When she came home at the end of January 1970, she was appalled at what a mess she had become – she who had always been so proper, prim, neat, fastidious. She had become a slug, a mess. She swore then, "NO more!" She went to

AA once or twice and then declared she couldn't stand listening to everyone's stories. No more, apparently she didn't need AA. Most people do.

In Mother's life and Bud and Judy's social circle, many parties were held every week. Between the Goldwaters and their crowd, and Bud and Judy's friends, there was always a party somewhere, and mother, being the great party gal, was always invited. At all these parties, the booze flowed freely. People did not know of her previous condition or her hospitalization for alcoholism, and we just kept it quiet. There was no need to discuss the issue.

Mother would go to parties with Bud and Judy, hold a full drink in her hand and not touch it. When either Bud or Judy finished their drink, they would take Mother's drink, hand her their empty glass and continue to drink their second one. When people came around offering to refill glasses, Mother would say, "No, thank you." But she would continue to hold the empty glass.

What stamina, what willpower! I always found that so amazing.

Mother did not take another drink for the remaining 16 years of her life until she was dying of throat cancer. Having been a two-pack a day smoker all her life, it was no wonder. The greatest wonder and blessing to me was the fact that once

Mother was sober, she and I became friends for the first time in our lives.

Once we moved to Scottsdale in 1974 and I was working for an electronics firm near where I lived, I visited her regularly every Wednesday. She looked forward to it. So did I. She was good company. She continued to smoke, which drove me crazy, but I figured my mother was worth whatever I had to endure.

ARIZONA – 1971

Business in Rockford went downhill in 1970. Rockford is a tool and die town, so when the country's business goes downhill, so does Rockford. It was a lovely place to live, and I just loved Roscoe, but no matter where you live one needs an income. Even though Tom's income went downhill, it appears that Bob Proctor still maintained his lifestyle.

We put our house on the market about November 1970. By December, we had a buyer, which meant we had to be out of the house December 31. I was making a ceramic nativity set, and it was a real rush to get all the pieces done, fired and painted. I still had to pack and to put stuff in storage and other stuff to take with us. It was a nightmare. I was so torn. I hated leaving the friends I had made, but I knew we had to move on. The ceramic Nativity now belongs to Tracy, my oldest daughter.

Tom decided that we would buy an eight-sleeper tent trailer and head west, trying to find work wherever possible. He already had several leads in Arizona. We packed up four kids and two dogs – Scamper the Beagle/Spaniel mix and Buttercup, our neurotic apricot Poodle. Living in an eight-sleeper tent trailer for two months with four kids, and two dogs was never my idea of fun. It only added to the nightmare.

So many friends gave us going-away parties. I'm just amazed when I think back on that time. God bless them all. They were such a great bunch of people. I remember Jeanne, Anne, and Martha. We had all done 4-H together. I kept a diary which details all those events, and the travels and travails we went through in moving so far away.

On our way west, we stopped in Jackson, Mississippi, to visit Tom's brother Bill and wife Woody and their two kids, Kim and Kirk. It was early January, but it was fun, kind of like Christmas only not so rushed as it was on December 25. It was fun to see them.

We proceeded west along the Gulf coast in early January 1971, stopping to visit friends in Houston for a couple days before continuing our journey into the unknown. Across Texas we went, camping in Big Bend National Park. We arranged a horseback ride with the kids while there. It was truly exciting, and the rangers were very informative. Standing high on a cliff overlooking the Rio Grande River was exciting. Going to sleep at night with coyotes howling all around us was like music. Big Bend National Park is truly one of the most spectacular national parks. It was an awesome adventure.

As we continued westward into New Mexico, we camped near Carlsbad Caverns. All of us were sick there at one time or another. It must have been some food we ate along the way. Because all of us were sick, we had to spend two or three days at Carlsbad. Tom went to the Caverns one day with two of the kids, and I went another day with the others, whoever wasn't sick at the moment. It was dreadful. There is nothing worse than being sick while on a road trip. However, the Caverns were awesome, and I'm glad we got a chance to see them.

We continued westward past El Paso, Las Cruces, and Deming into Arizona. Tom had some job leads in Arizona, and he decided that the best place to set up camp would be in the Phoenix area, as that is more centrally located.

Also, my mother was living in Scottsdale at the time. We figured we could find a trailer court somewhere in the Phoenix area. Boy! We sure didn't know the snowbird season in Arizona! There were no spots for trailers anywhere in the Phoenix area. We had to go clear out to Deer Valley, which was miles away, but that was all we could find.

We soon learned that the girls had to be in school. Truant officers came to our trailer one day. Well, end of the vacation for the Tracy and Karla. We spent six weeks stuck in that trailer park. The girls hated the school. They were teased and bullied. On top of that I had two kids left behind in the trailer every day with me, along with two dogs. It was a nightmare. The trailer park at least had decent bathrooms, for which I was grateful.

Campers are great for camping, but not very good for long-term living, especially with four kids and two dogs.

Tom had several interviews and job offers and finally decided to partner with a fellow in Tucson who had a metal building sales company. We immediately started looking for a house in Tucson, and Al, Tom's new partner, said we could stay with him until we found a house. We did find a place, on East 28th Street near Davis Monthan Air Base.

We quickly got moved in and gave up the camper life, for which I was grateful. Our furniture, having been in storage for almost two months, had to be hauled down to Tucson from Rockford.

The movers who were packing up our furnishings prior to our leaving Illinois packed a full can of garbage. I can't imagine their thinking. When we got all our furniture and furnishings out of storage and discovered the stinking full garbage can, I was appalled that movers would do such a thing!

As things turned out, many of our neighbors were airmen stationed at Davis Monthan. Stories of their flight duties and TDYs were truly fascinating to me, now seeing a different side of life from anything I'd experienced before.

We got to know these wonderful guys. We partied hearty, but what amazed me was the fellows who were scheduled for flight time or on call never drank a drop of anything alcoholic. What stamina, guts, and fortitude! Those guys were the cream of the crop!

We also discovered that they liked to camp and discovering our camper figured we were campers, too. Well, not really, but they introduced us to the most amazing camping spots in Arizona. We would spend three and four-day holiday weekends with this group and enjoyed them so much. While most of the country was enjoying, for instance, a typical Thanksgiving weekend around the dining table with roast turkey and all the fixin's, we were happily camping in some remote spot, grilling our meat on an open fire. Other food items rolled in tin foil were cooked on the hot coals, and even fishing early in the morning for breakfast. We had some great times. These were wonderful people and we had great times!

One time we camped by ourselves in the White Mountains over Labor Day weekend. We were hit with pelting rain and later with snow, the higher we got into the mountains. It was up near Big Lake.

Opening up the tent trailer, we discovered everything was wet because there was a huge leak in the roof. It was too late to go home, so we all slept in wet bedding. Sometime during the night a bear came crashing through our campsite, chased by some hound dogs. Scared me silly! A few minutes later we heard one of the dogs howl and screech in pain, but the dogs were still chasing the bear. I swore then that I'd never go camping in such wilderness again without a bear gun.

Another time we were camping at Madera Canyon with several friends. Late at night a gang of motorcyclists came roaring through the campsite without even slowing down. Bad manners – camping etiquette requires that when approaching or going through a campsite you cut your motors and walk your bike through the area before proceeding. And, this was pretty late – probably around 10:00 PM or so. Our big Field Spaniel mix dog, Scamper, tore after the riders and was kicked in the head by a girl riding anchor on one cycle. Scamper then took a big chunk out of her leg. The next morning the guys showed up – hippies, all except one airman.

All our friends scattered to their campers, hiding behind the curtained windows of their campers. They peered at me and the hippies, probably wondering what was going to happen to me. I walked out to meet these guys. No Fear! The hippies walked to me and told me they were going to sue me and report us to the Rangers for allowing a dog to roam loose. They looked pretty menacing, but for some reason, I was not afraid of them. You can stand up to bullies!

Heavens, everyone allowed their dogs to roam while in camp. Scamper was a good dog and very obedient. However, motorcyclists she did not like! I bluntly told them that they were way off base and didn't stand a chance and that they were at fault. I also noticed an airman in the group. Knowing that airmen would be punished by the military as well as civilian courts, I really let them have it.

However, they did report to the ranger, who then came to see us.

I told the ranger what had happened, and he claimed the hippies were at fault. When we got home from our trip, we already had a quarantine sign on our front door, and a sheriff's officer came to see us the next day. They found no fault with the dog's behavior and allowed us to keep the dog because our yard was securely fenced.

When Michael started school in Tucson in 1972, the teachers pretty much ignored him, stuck him in the back of the room where he would play with his Matchbox cars. Teacher would eventually confiscate the cars, producing them for me when we had Parent-Teacher conferences. One day he didn't show up in class, but no one called me for hours. We eventually found him on the playground inside a huge concrete pipe used as a play place for kids. He had his picture book and was quite happy.

Michael had some learning problems, had been diagnosed as borderline retarded, which teachers did not address. I was the one who patiently coached him through reading and math and other subjects. After a few years of struggling with reading, he finally got to the point where he loved to read. I was so proud of him!

While living in Tucson, I got bored with the daily coffee klatches and decided to do something else with my life. I got involved in an organization called "Meals on Wheels," or maybe it was "Mobile Meals," I don't remember. All I know is that this group had started the first in the nation delivering meals to shut-ins. They had a good routine worked out. We picked up food at the University of Arizona docks by the cafeteria. One cooler chest had hot food and the second one had cold food. The hot food was to be eaten immediately, and the cold food could be kept for a later snack or weekends when we did not deliver. Along with our designated food chests would be the list of homes to deliver.

I knew Tucson pretty well by this time, and the city was not very big, either. Some of those on my route were steady customers. Others would be on long enough to recuperate from illness or surgery. All were always glad to see us. We delivered meals five days a week – Monday through Friday. My day was Thursday. I got to know many of these people, and some became real friends. Sometimes when I got back to the dock to leave off the empty chests, I would find food still sitting waiting to be delivered. I would then deliver that route also. After I delivered my route, I would go back and visit my friends. Stella, you were something else! I loved you!

I volunteered at the Blind Center. I taught ceramics there, and it was truly great to see what people with vision impairment could do.

One of my food deliveries was a fellow who was technically blind, and whose wife had been recently committed because she had Alzheimers. She was in bad shape. However, once she was no longer around, the fellow fell into a morbid attitude. He would not do anything. I would even have to help him, with a template, sign his checks for bills due. For many months, I tried to get him to attend the blind center, but he kept refusing. The Center had a mini-bus that picked up people, so he didn't have to worry about transportation. Finally after months of my bugging him, he finally agreed to attend the blind center. It was a boon to him, and I was so glad to see that he finally agreed to move out into the world a bit.

Then, Tom's income fell drastically, and I ended up going back to work. It was not easy. Employers would look at my resume and ask if I "still knew how to type, or could I take shorthand?" It could have been humiliating, but I didn't let that annoy me. I knew I would face such situations.

I finally found a great boss. Ray Armstrong was President of Krueger Manufacturing Company, and he took a chance on me. Later on, a few months later, he told me I was the best secretary he ever had.

When Tom and Al parted company in 1974, I hated to leave. Ray Armstrong was such a kick and a great boss. He had lost a leg in WWII and would stump around on his peg leg. It bothered him terribly. At times, his pain was unbearable. Then, he would take a bottle of booze, a bottle of Percoset at home in hopes of getting through the night.

The next day he would show up at work (he never missed a day of work) wearing sunglasses. My gosh, his eyes were bloodshot! I told him more than once, "Ray, don't take off those sunglasses or you will bleed to death!" He was an amazing good sport, blunt, truthful, to the point, honest. He was the kind of boss worth working for. I shall never forget him. He had a John Wayne personality!

Ray Armstrong stood up for me. We had a customer who was particularly obnoxious and was rude to me on the phone. I hung up on him. I don't take that kind of treatment from anyone. I went immediately to Ray and told him what had happened. He told me to forward the customer's call to him the next time he called. Sure enough, the customer called a few minutes later. Ray read him the riot act. Turns out the customer had not paid his previous bills, which was the reason for the delayed shipment about which he was complaining. God bless bosses like Ray.

Scottsdale
1974

Tom found a job in Scottsdale, so we had to sell our house in Tucson, pack up the family and move again. We found a rental home in Scottsdale near an electronics plant, manufacturing parts for avionics systems for the government. The plant had the first GPS systems that went into satellites and ships at sea. Now everyone has GPS. Every space shot that ever went up had this company's equipment in it.

Initially, I found a job there working in Personnel. Now they call it HR – Human Relations. What other kind of relations are there? I got pretty bored working in HR and finally was able to transfer to the Materiel Department in Inventory Control. It was an excellent job. The position was like accounting, so I did well. We had our hands full tracking parts: from vendors, parts going through inspection, parts coming in from customers (some customers did supply some of their special parts),

parts in the Bond Room and parts in stock, and parts being moved to the production line. It was a good department to work in to see how the company and the production line functioned.

For a short period, I supervised an assembly line on a JPL project, I then transferred to Materiel Department as an Analyst, later moving into a Program Manager role for Materiel. It was demanding and hectic. My budgets for materiel and production were over $5 million for each project. These projects were in the late 1980s.

The older guys weren't too strict about government regulations. This was when strict OSHA regs were hitting the industry. We had many machine shops and plating shops in the plant. I knew them all well, as I was all over the plant in support of our programs. I'd have to go to the Bond Room, a plating shop, stockroom, to R&D, to graphics and who knows where else. When OSHA came along the older guys still kept dumping waste down the drain instead of into a holding tank. Managers there were reporting falsely to upper management, and the plant managers thought everything was going great. Then, the you-know-what hit the fan. Due to underground well testing EPA and OSHA discovered pollutions that apparently only this company could have caused. There were a couple other companies involved in the pollution, but the company stepped up and funded the money to clean the mess. What I learned is that a good manager has to know his area and make sure reporting is accurate and make sure his staff is doing things right. I learned a concept: Management by walking around!

In the "good old days" before we were inundated with government auditors and regulations, we would occasionally take one-hour lunch breaks and even more though the official lunch time was half an hour. Many people, mostly managers, would spend upwards of an hour in the cafeteria. We sometimes went out to lunch, especially for special events – someone's birthday, or just because it was Friday. Those lunches could end up being two hours, after a few brews and a long leisurely lunch. No one ever said anything. We would stay after work to make up the time.

Then the Defense Contract Administration Services (DCAS) started checking everyone's time cards. Auditors would stand at the front door of the building taking down everyone's name (we had to wear badges, of course) and noting the time we left the building. If we weren't back within half an hour, they would come check our time cards and dock us time. If we falsified our time card, we were in big trouble. It got pretty ugly. The auditing got so bad we could hardly leave the plant and go across the street, order lunch, eat and get back to the plant under half an hour.

After so many years of working in the Materiel Department, Contract Management beckoned. After taking specialized courses and passing the rigorous exam, I became an official Contract Manager. It was exciting working contracts with the government. What I learned was that DCAA (Defense Contract Audit Agency) agents didn't know much about what they were inspecting in reviewing our documents. It always seemed they were there to harass us more than anything. Some of the Contract Managers were less than honest with us younger people. We would end up doing ALL the work on a contract, negotiating back and forth with the customer for months before we had it all put together. When it was time to do the final negotiations, we sat on the sidelines and were told to keep our mouths shut. I was appalled at their behavior. And – some of the managers were extremely chauvinistic! The older Contract Managers in the office would often send me to deal with DCAA because the auditors could be so difficult. The contracts I worked were principally for the Army located in Rock Island, Illinois.

Less than a year after working in the Contract Management Department, new government regulations and laws caused us to lose many of our contracts. We lost most of our contracts with the government. Congress had made massive changes in contract law. Little did Congress know about contracts! My good job was gone!

Being one of the last hired in Contracts, I was one of the first let go, but then ended up in the Computer Networking Department. They were just beginning to computerize their staff and communications. For some reason the company felt I knew more about computers than most – I had years earlier taken several computer programming language courses. I learned Cobol, Fortran, Basic and other languages I've since forgotten. That was fun – we had to produce our batch of punch cards, and then feed them into a gigantic card-reading machine and hope our program worked. I decided not to go into full-time computer programming because of the weird schedules that could happen if a computer disaster occurred.

I was working in Personnel several years prior, when a new payroll system was being rolled out. It fell in the tank. Many people got negative paychecks. Can you imagine getting a check for -$600 instead of a +$600? Everything came unglued, and the programmers were ordered to stay in the computing center until they solved the problem! It took them two or three days to redo the payroll program. Those programmers were good guys, though, and I learned a lot from them.

In Computer Networking, they named me "System Administrator." I said, "system what?" I soon learned and had a steep learning curve. Again, I had lots of good help, and many technical classes to attend. Novell was the software language we used, and my network had five in-line RAID servers.

One day my server was doing strange things and dropping users' files. I called in some tech experts after failing to solve the problem myself. Poor guys – they spent all day working on that server, removing and replacing one part after another. Nothing solved the problem! Finally, in desperation they checked the cable connection, and that was the problem. Moral: Always check your connections before anything else. After all that work the tech engineers decided to leave all the new parts in the server, so I had a brand new server.

One of the fun things I had to do as a System Administrator was to load all the proper software on each user's new computer. The software included Mail, Word, Excel, PowerPoint and our security programs. After configuring each computer, I delivered the computer to each user.

Often, the response I got upon delivering a computer was something like, "What in the world is that thing?" The language they used to me was often unprintable. They would often refuse to use it. These were high paid managers who spent their lives travelling back and forth to Washington and often overseas. Few had ever used a computer. These men were no dummies; they just weren't used to computers or what to do with them, nor did they want to take their valuable time to learn these new monstrosities.

I explained that I would set up a time to work with them to teach them the basics. They also would attend classes for each software program. Their biggest problem was learning how to incorporate mail and the other programs, and how to attach a file and how to use their calendar. Our calendaring system worked such as a boss would have the ability to force a meeting onto their calendars.

I had to explain that ALL communications would be coming henceforth via email to their computers, so they HAD to learn computers. It was a tough learning curve for some as they travelled so much. The word came down from top managers that all meetings henceforth would be PowerPoint presentations. No more handing out

20 copies each of a 20-page report. I liked this. So much easier, and it saved reams of paper.

I often had to go to users' homes to install security software so they could access our computer systems remotely. We had two firewalls, and they were well guarded. One of my jobs was to add users' names to the firewall software. Also, I had to program their laptops to work securely no matter where in the world they were. Laptops then were huge clunky affairs, weighing maybe 15 pounds; upon returning to the office, the laptops went into docking stations and became regular desktop computers.

Our department was overhead, so none of the work we did for someone was a direct charge, except if a user caused damage.

One manager came back from a trip, gave me his laptop computer, said it didn't work and would I please fix it. I took it back to the lab, and the tech guys and I opened it up and immediately smelled sweet creamed coffee. Oooops! Looks like this guy did some damage. I went back and told him what we found, and he sheepishly admitted that the plane he was on hit an air pocket while he was working on the computer with a cup of coffee in one hand. Not a good thing to do on an airplane. We had to charge his department, unfortunately.

Another person was a department secretary whose husband was a game developer. She kept bringing games to install on her company computer after everyone knew they couldn't do that.

The game software would play havoc with the computer systems, and her computer would quit working. I'd remove the bad software and get the computer running perfectly again. After several episodes like this we had to tell her that we were going to inform her boss if she didn't quit installing game software. We finally had to charge her department for the time we spent, and we had to inform her boss that she was violating company policy.

I had about 200 users on my network. They really kept me hopping. I did have three or four other Techs working with me, but it was still hectic. I also had to deal with upper management on the third floor. When they called, everything else had to be dropped. Other users with problems hated that. I didn't much blame them. I finally opted for less hectic and more structured environment and moved into the Computer Security area, where we dealt with security software, passwords, and remote access.

When I started working at this company in the 1970s, I finished my Bachelor's Degree at

Arizona State University and the University of Phoenix. In later years, I got advanced training and certification in computer networking and design in the 1980s.

Apache Junction
1977
Miracles DO Happen

After 20 years of living with Tom and enduring the stress and infidelity and his brutality against me, and finally the children, I decided I could take no more and called it quits.

Tom wasn't working, hadn't worked for almost a year, and we were living on his unemployment check and what little I earned at the time. Things were getting rough. He was home and drinking all the time. I had no idea what might be going on. When he drank, he got uglier by the minute. One day I walked in to see him slugging the girls. I had enough! That was it. No more! I told him to get out (in some very strong language), and he crept out of the room like a scalded dog. I also informed him and the kids I was leaving. I asked the kids if they wanted to go with me or stay with their Dad – their choice.

They all four of them came running after me as I was walking down the hallway, screaming, "Don't leave us behind, don't leave us with Dad!" I never realized life with Tom was so bad for the children.

The next day I located a lawyer, explained the situation to him. He found a judge who expedited my divorce and the final decree. Now my big issue was to get Tom out of the apartment. He begged me, came crawling, literally, to not kick him out, and how dare I divorce him. I was his wife. He said I couldn't do such a thing. My reply was something like, "Watch me!" He was OK – he moved in with his girlfriend in the next apartment.

My next big issue was to find a place to live. It was the middle of the month; our rent was good until the end of the month. That was it. Beyond that, there was nowhere to go. Period.

I looked into Federal Housing in the Phoenix area, and it was pretty gruesome, especially with four children, ages 11 to 17. I had to find something else.

I mentioned my quandary to my best friend, Joyce, at lunch the next day. She remarked that on the way to work each day as she drove down McKellips Road in Mesa, there was a big billboard with information pertaining to government homes.

On my lunch hour the next day, I drove out to Mesa, where I'd never been, found the billboard, pulled over and wrote down all the information on it. Getting back to work, I called the realtor's listed phone number, which I found on the billboard. He answered and upon hearing my problem, said, "Yes, I have three homes left in Apache Junction. If you meet me after work, I can show them to you."

I wanted to scream "Apache Junction????" The armpit of the valley. Nothing good ever came out of Apache Junction (as far as I knew). I quickly realized that beggars cannot be choosers, and my lot was not exactly on top of humanity's heap right now. We had been living in Scottsdale and Phoenix; Mesa, east of the Valley, and Apache Junction, up against the Superstition Mountains, was foreign territory to me.

I asked the realtor (I've since forgotten his name, but he and his wife were marvelous people – they both helped me so much) how to get to his office. When he told me his location was at Recker Road and Main Street in Mesa, I didn't have a clue how to get there, but I soon found out.

Getting to his office after work, he took me out to see the three homes he had left in his inventory of government homes. They were all government-subsidized homes, built under the Department of Agriculture for Farmers Home Administration (commonly called FmHA, as opposed to FHA which is the Federal Housing Authority). FmHA built homes in rural areas, and I guess Apache Junction at the time was considered rural.

Two of the homes the realtor showed me were decent enough on the inside, but on dirt streets with chain link enclosed commercial properties next door. There were no zoning codes in Apache Junction at the time – you could build anything you wanted wherever you wanted.

The third house the realtor showed me was a dollhouse. On a real, paved street (a rarity in Apache Junction), with curbs and sidewalks, in a nice neighborhood with similar houses. Local contractors had built them well, to government specifications. At that time, local realtors sold or handled the sale of the government FmHA homes. The Agriculture Department (FmHA) changed that policy in later years.

I chose this third house he showed me. The realtor informed me that the house had just come back on the market that morning, after another couple failed to qualify for it. Telling me that the house would probably move pretty fast, he took me back to his office where I filled out a ton of paperwork. Then, the best of all, his wife would take the paperwork to the government office the next day. She would have to be there very early, about 4:00 AM, in order to be the first in line. If anyone else would have been in line ahead of her and wanted the same house, I would have been out of luck. As luck would have it, and thanks to the realtor's wife, she was the first in line.

The government agent informed her that my paperwork seemed to be in order, and it looked like I was quite eligible for this house.

The government agent then brought me in to interview me. He went over all the paperwork, asking questions, verifying answers. Then, I dropped the bomb on him: Could I move in before the end of the month, before closing, as I had no place to go with four children?

He said that was quite unusual, had never been done before, but since my paperwork seemed to be in good order, he OK'd me to move in before final closing. Then, he warned me, saying, "But, if anything in your paperwork turns out to be false, you will have to move out." I was not worried, knowing that all that bundle of paper had nothing but the truth in it.

I moved in, even getting help from my ex-husband and teenage kids. It was minimal housing. We had beds for the five of us, plus a hand-me-down kitchen table and living room couch. But we were fine and had a substantial roof over our heads. This little house had real air conditioning, not the proverbial swamp cooler common in desert climates. Thank heavens!

The house was 1000 square feet with four bedrooms and two bathrooms, and a tiny kitchen with all the counter space on one wall, and barely room enough for a table and chairs and refrigerator. That was OK with me.

There was no shower in the main bathroom, so the kids were coming into my bathroom every night to shower. It could get pretty steamy, especially in the summer. Finally, Tommy, my oldest son, rigged up a shower from the bathtub faucet, but there was no tile on the wall, just wallboard. Soon, the wallboard began to disintegrate. What did we expect? Then, I went to the hardware store, bought tile and grout and a special cutter, and tiled the space around the tub myself. First, I had to repair the disintegrated wallboard. I did a pretty good job if you ask me.

Then, I called a plumber to put in a real showerhead, and we had a real bathroom then. After the tile around the tub, I figured I could tile the floor also. That wasn't too difficult but didn't realize that when tiling the floor, you have to remove the toilet first. I didn't do that, but otherwise the tile looked very good. I've always wondered what subsequent owners thought when they went to perhaps re-tile the bathroom.

While living there barely a year, my silver and turquoise jewelry was stolen, along with a jewel box my aunt (who was an artist) had made for me when I was a little kid. I was so upset because I realized that my son, Mike, had probably stolen it, or his friends (who weren't really friends – they just used him). I called the police, and they came and inspected everything and declared it to be an inside job.

The two friends of Mike were terrible delinquents. I had told them repeatedly that they were NOT allowed in the house, but every day when I got home from work, there they were, brazenly sitting in my living room. I had told Mike quite strongly that NO ONE was to be in the house when I wasn't home. He was such a pushover for those brats.

OK – I had a chest full of sterling flatware, a wedding gift that I no longer used. I sold it and bought myself a piano. The price of silver had reached new highs. How I enjoyed that piano. It gave me joy for many years, much more so than a chest of silver stuck away in a drawer somewhere.

There was a shed outside that had hookups for washer and dryer, but since we couldn't afford a washer or dryer, I had to go to the Laundromat on weekends. Tommy and I rigged up laundry lines so I could hang the clothes to dry, thereby saving me some laundry money. Besides which, I enjoy hanging out laundry. Everything, especially sheets, smells so fresh.

As time went on, I landscaped the front and back yard, added fencing, gravel in the front yard, and desert landscaping in the back, with a small green patch for the dogs. I did all the work myself, with occasional slave labor from Tommy and his teenage friends. What are friends for?

My back yard was beautiful. Friends would come to sit and enjoy the peaceful atmosphere. I so enjoyed that yard. Mother would always give me money for birthdays and other occasions, telling me to spend the money on myself. Invariably I would buy another tree or shrub. The back yard had a big palm tree, an Australian Bottle tree, and peach trees. Along the south fence I planted century plants. I planted pomegranates, grape and tomato vines. Desert broom (a real mess and hard to get rid of) bloomed "voluntarily." A huge poinsettia against the white slump block of the house was eave high and six feet wide and had come from a Christmas poinsettia some years back. I even planted a watermelon vine in the palm tree well, and when the watermelon grew up, it grew UP! Right into the branches of the palm tree. Have you ever seen watermelon hanging from a palm tree?

I noticed that one repossessed house next door had fencing around it. I called the government agent and asked him why I couldn't also have fencing around my house? He claimed that fencing was a later thing and that at the time I moved in the government wasn't doing fencing. However, he informed me that if I wanted to add the cost to my mortgage, I was welcome to do that. He informed me I would have to get three bids and submit them to his office; after he approved one of them, the work could begin.

After the fence was done, the neighbor on the other side decided to fence his yard, and I agreed to let him hook into my fence. After all, it was all government property, wasn't it?

The whole scenario of obtaining a decent house in Apache Junction was a series of miracles: finding the billboard; finding the realtor; the house coming back on the market the day I was looking at houses; the government agent allowing me to move in before closing; Mother's gifts of money for trees and shrubs.

Every day after work, I would sit on my front porch. There I had a gorgeous view of the Superstition Mountains and the "alpenglow" of the sunset against the sheer granite cliff sides of the mountain. I thanked God every single day of my life that I had such a beautiful place to live.

The Clandestine Party Next Door

After the fencing had been completed, I planted an entire row of century plants on the south fence side next to my other neighbor. They grew up to be pretty big. They are wicked plants, with huge spikes at the end of each blade. One night, the lady next door was out of town with her boyfriend. Her two kids, ages 12 and 14, left at home alone, decided to have a party. Teenage boys bought two kegs of beer, and the whole school was invited. The party got quite raucous. Upon investigating the noise and clatter, I discovered our whole cul-de-sac was totally blocked with cars and the house was jumping. I went in and called the cops and was told I was the second person to call, and the cops were on their way. I pulled a lawn chair onto the driveway and decided to wait for the fun to begin! Soon, the cops showed up, and a few kids out front yelled, "Cheez-it, the cops!" Then the scurrying began. Kids burst from that house in all directions. A bunch of them came over my fence into the century plants. I can't imagine the wounds and scars they must have acquired in the process, and how they explained to their parents. The next day, the lady blamed me for "spoiling her weekend." Oh, Really? The two kids who lived there had no place to go, so they were picked up. Many of the other kids managed to get away, but the cops did pick up several of them.

When Tommy was old enough to get a job, he had to have a waterbed. Fine with me – it was his money. The waterbed barely fit in his bedroom. The dresser was a real squinch, but he had his waterbed.

When I first moved to Apache Junction, I was still paying off bills that my ex was supposed to pay. Creditors could never find him, so they came after me. They cared nothing about a divorce decree. I ended up getting a second job at Walgreens to pay off bills.

That's where I met my friend, Shannon, who raised Shelties. She and her roommate were going on vacation and asked if I would house and dog sit. I did, and they gave me one of their Shelties from their latest litter. Misty was a beautiful Sheltie. I trained her well and never had to have her on a leash, unless we went over town where the crowds were. Down the street we would go. She would wait at the curb for me and when I said, "OK," away she would go. Getting across the street to the desert, she took off – all I could see of her was the tail waving above the chaparral. When Tommy left home to live in his own apartment, he would come by after work and pick her up and take her to the lake with him. When I found Misty missing, I knew where she was. She loved to go to the lake with us, and wouldn't stay on the beach, but would swim out to our boat. She loved the water. I still miss her. Shelties are grand dogs. She would herd our other dogs. I often had three or four dogs, depending on what the kids brought home.

We had beautiful lakes on the Salt River System. All the lakes were part of the Salt River Project Power System, which produced electric power for the Valley (the "Valley" was the total of Phoenix and all the surrounding cities). Saguaro Lake was the first lake, Apache Lake the second one and Roosevelt Lake the third and the highest one in the chain of lakes. We did a lot of swimming, boating and fishing on those lakes. For family get-togethers, we would rent cabins at Apache Lake. Apache Lake was a good place to go because it was more remote than Saguaro and Roosevelt, and had cabins for overnight rentals. The big problem was getting there. From the south, we could take Fish Creek Hill, which was truly hazardous, or from the north, go by way of Roosevelt Lake and south from there, a very long way to go. Fish Creek Hill was murderous. It was narrow, one-lane, literally carved out of the vertical cliffside, no fencing or guard rails of any kind. As the road deteriorated over time, spikes were driven horizontally into the side of the hill, so vehicles would often be driving with their wheels on the spikes sticking out of the cliffside. Not exactly my cup of tea! Vehicles going up the steep hill had the right of way; those going downhill had to pull over and wait for the upcoming vehicles to pass.

One day I was driving home, on an uphill stretch, and a huge motorhome (what was this guy thinking???) was coming downhill. We met, with no way to pass. I got out of my car and walked over to the driver, and told him that downhill vehicles were supposed to pull over and wait for uphill vehicles to pass. He just snorted at me, with a line of cars behind him, and said "Sorry lady, I can't back up." I also had a line of vehicles behind me, but we all had to back down this treacherous hill. I was not thinking pleasant thoughts at the time.

Every time we went to Apache Lake by way of Fish Creek Hill, we would see another car over the side about a thousand feet down. At times, the

State Troopers and helicopters would be there, attempting another rescue.

This road belonged to the Salt River Project, not the State Park System. There was no way this road would ever be widened.

As my income increased, so did my house payment to the government. I didn't mind, I figured that was only fair. Finally, they told me I could no longer have a government loan at all, due to my income increases, and would have to finance the house in the commercial market. That, too, seemed only fair to me. I had several years of subsidized mortgage payments, but now I could pay my way. This was a time when interest rates on loans had skyrocketed to heights not seen since. Not fun!

Mother died in 1986, leaving my brother and me a small amount of money from her estate. By that time, my beautiful neighborhood was beginning to deteriorate something awful. Apartments near us were being rented through HUD, and consequently HUD was putting the poorest of the poor in those apartments. Those people had no care for the property, children or pets. Children ran around naked, pets ran loose with no licensing, garbage was thrown out the windows, and the kids were incorrigible! Kids were siphoning gas from my gas tank, and another blew out a kitchen window with a ball bat, and kids were constantly throwing rocks at my dogs in the back yard. Every time we had to mow the lawn, I had first to clean up all the rocks in the yard. It was time to move, especially since my three oldest children had moved out, leaving just me and Mike.

But, since living in Apache Junction, my life there had been one miracle after another. How else could I explain what I was able to do on what my salary was (at that time)? Miracles DO happen! How else do I explain obtaining the house that I did? I had lived there for ten and a half years, and they were good years. I left there in December 1987.

One day, four or five of us were traveling to Tucson for a DAR meeting. I was driving as I had a big enough van to accommodate everyone. We were taking the "back way" into Tucson – along the Superstition Mountains and the scenic byways you don't see from the I-10 freeway. It is a nice drive and a bit quicker as that route has less traffic. I had one more person to pick up before turning south to Tucson. Coming to a four-way stop in the rural area east of Apache Junction, I came to a stop. Looking every which way there were no cars, except for one about a mile away, off to my right. I turned left to go north and all of a sudden I felt my van being "shoved" or "moved" into the southbound left turn lane. As I sat there dumbfounded as to why or how this could happen, a car (the one I had seen in the far distance) came whistling by doing about 100 miles per hour (the speed limit was 45 or 50 mph.). This was phenomenal. If we had been in the northbound lane the resulting crash would have been disastrous! Another miracle!

1986

Mother was dying of throat cancer. She had smoked two packs of cigarettes a day her whole life. There was no more we could do. The doctors did some radiation treatments, but that was not helping. It was time to let her go.

Once the throat cancer set in, there was not much my brother or I could do. She was in constant pain and wanted some strong whiskey to kill the pain. Bud and I agreed that considering the situation it was probably the best thing we could do for her. She also refused to go to a nursing home, preferring to stay in the only home she and Dad had ever owned. Bud and I shrugged our shoulders and figured we would find her dead someday, and there's nothing else can be done. The remarkable thing is that she was able to care for herself until the day she died. Bud did find her, September 18, 1986. She was then 77 years old.

Only a couple days before, Mother told me to shop for whatever I wanted for my birthday (the 20th of September), and she would reimburse me the money. I never found just what I wanted, so I never bought anything. I stopped by Tom and Di's house on my way home that evening September 18, 1986 to see them briefly, and they told me everyone was looking for me that Mother had died earlier that day. Tom and Di were living in Mesa, and I was still living in Apache Junction.

Her funeral service was the Order of Eastern Star and she was buried next to Dad in the Masonic section of Greenwood Memorial in Phoenix.

Mesa
Fountain of the Sun
December 1987

I sold my house in Apache Junction in December 1987 moved to Fountain of the Sun, an adult community, in Mesa. I found a lovely split bedroom home with large kitchen and formal dining area, two full baths and large back yard and huge patio about 40 feet by 15 feet across part of the back of the house. It was a nice sized 1200 square feet home.

It was here that I got involved in Republican politics, at first a precinct worker, then precinct chairman, then district secretary. I made many friends there, and they were the ones urging me to become politically active. We all were active – ringing doorbells, making phone calls, etc. It never ended.

I was working for the Republican Party when John McCain first came into Arizona looking for a state from which to run for Congress. He took the seat of a retiring Representative, and two years later ran for the Senate. He's been there ever since. I've never met anyone who liked the guy and could never figure out how he keeps getting reelected. He was arrogant and had the habit of not returning phone calls, messages or replying to letters. However, Jon Kyl was a superb Senator, and I always appreciated communications with him. John McCain waltzed into Republican headquarters in Phoenix one day when he first arrived in Arizona and started giving orders to everyone, like he owned the joint. We all stood around dumbfounded at such arrogance.

My youngest son, Mike, was 22 years old and I knew he couldn't live on his own yet, so he came with me to Fountain of the Sun. Rules stated that the homeowner had to be 50 or older, and anyone younger living with me had to be over 18. It worked out pretty well. Mike was attending some special classes at Mesa Community College and appeared to be doing OK. I would often pick him up when I left work, so it worked out well.

When I first moved to Fountain of the Sun, the freeway eastbound ended at Gilbert Road, which was a few miles west of us. After a few years, the freeway got extended to beyond our development and the entrance/exit was right near our house. Traffic by our house increased to tens of thousands of cars a day, and the pollution was not only dirtying my house, but also causing me agonizing asthma problems. Time to move again.

THE NAVAJOS - 1990S

One Sunday our church service included an impassioned plea from a member of a Navajo tribe at Indian Wells, Arizona. This was a small tribe about a half-hour drive north of Holbrook, Arizona. Their small native church had burned to the ground the previous week and they had no funds to rebuild. Since this was a Presbyterian church, members of the tribe were making the rounds of the Presbyterian churches in Arizona asking for funds to rebuild.

Their most pressing need was contractors. Navajo people were primarily sheep herders and had no knowledge of basic construction. Coordinating with other churches in Arizona, we began the arduous process of finding contractors willing to drive the four hours to Indian Wells on weekends or their spare time to help the Indian Wells people.

We found electricians, roofers, carpenters, dry wallers, tilers and lots of construction people, but could not locate a commercial plumber, someone who knew infrastructure and could read blueprints. Construction could not begin before the ditches were dug and basic lines were laid for plumbing, electrical, sewage, etc. We prayed and prayed and put notices everywhere. No luck for many weeks, though we had other contractors lined up.

One night I was sitting at my computer, when the phone rang. I answered it, and a man asked, "Is this Kaye Morgan?" My first response was, "Are you a plumber?" He was astonished and said, "How did you know I am a plumber?

This man became the lead in establishing the first phase of construction. Being a commercial construction plumber, he knew how to read blueprints and how to communicate with other contractors and the Indians on what needed to be done and how to establish infrastructure. He would eventually drive four hours to Indian Wells early Saturday morning, put in eight hours and drive home that evening. On Sunday he did the same, sometimes taking his children with him. He did this every weekend for months, until the basic construction phase was over. Then, he helped regular plumbers install fixtures and appliances inside. His dedication, without pay, was astonishing.

A local mining operation donated ditch digging equipment. Many contractors donated their time, without pay, as did the plumber who called me.

Churches all over Arizona donated time, money, Navajo language Bibles and hymnals, pews and other furniture for the sanctuary, furnishings for the fellowship hall, paintings, art work and much more.

During my time spent there, I got to know the Navajo people. They are magnificent, among the most spiritual people I've known. I was privileged to share meals with them, to meet the elders and "talk" with them. The older people speak only Navajo, the younger ones speak both Navajo and English, so it was through them that I could talk with the Elders.

These people have so little, barely more than a roof over their heads, yet they are a happy and satisfied people. Here, I'm talking about the Christian population of the Navajos. About half are Christian, the other half adhere to the "old" ways and their spirit gods and medicine men. Poverty is endemic. Many years ago the Tribal Council voted to cut sheep numbers in half because the number of sheep were denuding the lands and creating widespread desertification, making matters worse by the year. The Navajo count their wealth in sheep or horses. One horse is worth two sheep. Having to give up half their herd drove these people deeper into poverty.

At last, after many months, the church was built and ready to be dedicated. This new church at Indian Wells had indoor plumbing, electricity, gas, a real kitchen, dishwasher, stove and other appliances for the fellowship hall, all donated by various churches in Arizona. The old church was a simple adobe structure with a fireplace to heat the one room in winter. It burned to the ground, leaving a blackened spot. Indians will not go near where a fire destroyed a building. We then had to find a spot nearby that was suitable for their new church.

During the dedication ceremony, representatives from all the other churches were there to take part. To my astonishment, I was presented with a plaque honoring the work I had done. I didn't do that much – I was the "coordinator" and heavy-duty "pray"-er.

One of the problems the Navajos now had was that they had no income to afford the electric, water and gas bills to support their new church. Now began the visits to Washington by college-educated Navajos to get money that was due the tribe. The Bureau of Indian Affairs (BIA) was long ago charged with keeping money in trust for the various Indian tribes. It appeared that not much of the money was ever given or spent on the tribes. Now the latter generation of Navajos was tasked with trying to pry money out of Washington to help support the tribe.

Working with and getting to know the Navajos was one of the greatest moments of my life. It was a profound experience.

FOUNTAIN HILLS - 1998

I moved to Fountain Hills in 1998 just a few months before I retired early. After looking at various "clean air" communities around Arizona, I had to make up my mind. I didn't want to be too far from Tom and Di – they were such fun to be with and my only child still in Arizona – the other three were in California.

While living in Fountain Hills for six years I made many friends there and occasionally got a chance to play golf with friends who lived there.

I organized a new DAR (Daughters of the American Revolution) chapter, which we named Four Peaks Chapter. The name came from the famous Four Peaks of the Superstition Mountains which loom over and are part of the Fountain Hills landscape.

While a member of the Four Peaks Chapter DAR, I became a "National Memorial Lady." This is a special designation of those who attend veterans' burial ceremonies at National Memorial

Grave sites. The National Memorial Cemetery in the area was actually in Cave Creek. Our duty as a National Memorial lady was to attend the service, to attend the grieving, to present the family with any reminisces from friends. All the services produced tears. The worst were the Vietnam veterans. It seems that so many of them were deaths due to drugs and suicide, which is so awful. Many older veterans from World War II or the Korean War had no family to represent them, so we ladies were there to be their representative. Being a National Memorial lady was one of my fondest memories, but also the saddest. I never failed to feel truly blessed by being a part of these ceremonies. A twenty-one gun salute volley was fired at each ceremony. I was given a shell casing from one of the gun salutes. I still have it. It reminds me of my service to our veterans. But, it is a sad memory.

Fountain Hills was next to the Verde River Valley, consequently we had wildlife galore to be marveled over. There were Great Blue Herons, which stood as high as my shoulder, eagles which nested in the cliffs bordering the Verde River, and many other birds. There was other wildlife, many pests such as peccaries (or javelina), skunks and coyotes. The javelina were the worst. They ate all kinds of flowers. Some people gave up and put in artificial flowers. They supposedly did not eat geraniums, so I planted geraniums on my patio. One night they came by and uprooted all of them.

One night I heard a terrible ruckus on my patio, and looking out the glass door to see what was going on, I saw a tribe of about a dozen javelina. They were merrily munching away on some dog food that I had put up on a shelf. They had dragged it down to the floor and tore into it with wild abandon. Not knowing what to do to get rid of these monsters, I called the sheriff's office. They told me to turn on the light and bang some pots and pans, that the critters didn't like noise. I did just that, and they all looked at me and went back to merrily munching away. I called the sheriff again and this time a deputy came out with a huge powerful spotlight. That made them go away, but not far. With the searchlight shining brightly, the little monsters retreated to around the corner of the building. I could see their noses sticking out, checking to see what we were doing. The deputy helped me to clean up the dog food, which I then put in the shed. Lesson learned.

The Sheriff warned us to not go walking alone at night, as both javelina and coyotes traveled in packs at night and could be dangerous if they are in packs. I did my walking during the day, as much as I always loved walking at night. In other places where I lived, I often went walking at night and often came across wild animals – skunks and coyotes mostly, but they were never a big problem, as in Fountain Hills.

I was coming home late one evening. I parked my van in the garage and was walking along the sidewalk to my condo when I met a huge pack of javelina. I quickly retreated up the stairs of the condo nearest me and waited for the monsters to pass. Boy! Did they stink, another of their peculiar attributes! Our condo development was open to the desert with no surrounding wall or barrier of any kind, so any wild critter could wander through our yards.

In another instance, a lady was walking her little dog past a vacant field where there was a huge area of brush where coyotes often resided. One coyote came rushing out, grabbed the little dog and retreated to the brushy compound, leash and all. The poor lady stood there horrified.

I watched young coyotes one day attempt to play tag with a big dog being walked by a fellow. The dog was part Great Dane and part something else, but nevertheless the young coyote wanted to play. He would entice the dog toward the brush area, and the dog would follow. The fellow would call the dog back. The coyote came out of the brush again, and again the dog followed him toward the brush and the fellow called the dog back. After I watched for some time, I finally walked off. I later learned that coyotes, working as a pack, would entice a dog or some other critter attempting to play with them, and when the animal got close enough, other coyotes would pounce on it. Clever animals. Don't trust coyotes!

I was always careful to keep my dog close to me when I walked through this area.

One day I discovered Gambel Quail eggs in a huge flower pot on the pot shelf on the patio. Every day another egg was there. After about a dozen eggs had been laid, the female started to sit on the eggs. Sometimes the male would relieve her for a while. After about three weeks, the eggs began to hatch, and pretty much all at once, too. I wasn't sure what to do about little quail dropping off the pot shelf onto the cement patio, so I called the Extension Service at the University (ASU). They told me to put a blanket on the patio, but not to worry as baby quail have a very tough breastbone which prevents any injury when taking a fall like this. I watched as the eggs hatched, one by one. The mother quail was across the yard (desert landscaping) calling to them. I had never heard such a call from a quail. The little ones dropped off the pot shelf one by one and went running to the mother who was calling them. After all twelve hatched, and she had gathered them all, she went trotting off across the landscape trailing twelve little ones. Quail are "precocious," meaning they can walk as soon as they hatch. Chickens are also precocious. Other birds have to be nursed for several days or weeks before they can leave the nest. They are called "altricial."

I observed these quail for several days. Every day or so, another would be missing. The mother quail never nested in the same spot each night. The last I saw of this family there were three birds left.

One night I was watching TV. The blinds on the sliding glass door to the patio were open. I looked up and saw five Ringtails with their noses pressed against the glass door, looking at me. Fascinated, I watched them for several minutes, then as one they turned and walked away. I had never seen Ringtails before and thought they were Raccoons. I mentioned them to my daughter-in-law's father a few days later. He informed me they were Ringtails. Although Raccoons abound pretty much everywhere in this country, they are not found in the Sonoran Desert. Here we had Ringtails, a cousin to the pesky Raccoons. And, yes, Ringtails are pesky, too. Most farmers will try to get rid of them.

I also got involved with the Chamber of Commerce while living in Fountain Hills. I was a "Purple People" helper when the Chamber staged their two art festivals every year. Fountain Hills held one festival in November and one in February. Both festivals consisted of juried vendors from around the country who tried yearly to be included in these festivals. We Purple People wore huge purple sashes across our chests (that's why we were called "Purple People"), indicating that we were part of the Chamber helpers. We were there to help the vendors with whatever they needed. Sometimes we would buy their lunch, or sit their booth while they took a break. We usually worked three-hour shifts. It was great fun, and we Purple People got to meet people from around the country.

The second art festival was in February and included the Balloon Festival, where there were balloon races from Fountain Hills to some designated spot in the Valley. (The area surrounding Phoenix and its 30 or so suburbs was known as the "Valley of the Sun," or the "Valley"). This festival was like the November one, and we Purple People worked it also.

These festivals took over the whole downtown area, as vendors' booths lined both sides of all the streets. Food vendors and musicians were at every intersection, so we always had a great choice of food and music to enliven the atmosphere. Great fun!

While living in Fountain Hills I got involved with the Desert Botanical Garden. It is next to the zoo on Galvin Parkway near the airport.

I loved volunteering at the Garden, later becoming Day Captain for the Thursday Docents. What fun it was to lead tours through the Garden, enlightening people on desert vegetation and Indian culture and how the ancient people used everything.

One of my favorite things to do was to work the *Las Noches de las Luminarias*, (or "the Night of the Lights") starting at Thanksgiving and ending at Christmas. All the pathway luminarias had to be lighted by hand before our official shift started at 5:00 PM. I liked this shift better than the later shift that was from about 7 PM to 10 PM. The later shift had to put out all the candles in the luminarias when the Garden closed. The early shift had the advantage of always a stupendous sunset. The sunset, viewed from the Garden, was a sight to delight the soul. A couple of years that I worked this festival, we had the Chihuly Glass Exhibit. The glass exhibits were awesome, and camera shots of the various sculptures do not do them justice. Information about Chihuly sculptures can be viewed at chihuly.com. During *Las Noches de las Luminarias* the whole Garden was lit up with luminarias lining all the pathways and lights strung about our heads, and the Chihuly glass exhibits lit up. It was like a fairyland. There were booths scattered about that sold beer, wine, and whiskey, so everyone was happy. We were certainly not allowed to go near those booths while working or wearing our official badges. There were various music groups staged throughout the Garden. With the lights and music and all the happy people, it was a delightful venue to work. For more information, go to dbg.org.

I loved Fountain Hills, but when I constantly had a scratchy throat, I had to investigate what was causing the problem. Research led me to the ozone problem in Phoenix and the Ozone Maps available on the Internet. Ozone is created in the downtown area of Phoenix due to all the traffic and at the airport. There is not enough prevailing breeze to take away the ozone. It drifts northeasterly and lodges in the hills surrounding Fountain Hills and Rio Verde. Time to move again.

Back to Mesa again.

Mesa, Arizona
2004 To 2009
Leisure World

I moved back to Mesa, looking for a condo, but with my little dog, there were no condos available to me. I ended up buying a house in Leisure World, a guard-gated 55+ community about one and a half square miles and 2700 homes. Fortunately, this home was away from the major traffic and faced north, so I didn't get the brunt of traffic pollution.

While living in Mesa, both this time, and when living at Fountain of the Sun, I belonged to Church of the Master, a large Presbyterian church in Mesa. I served several terms as a Deacon and at times was Moderator of the Board of Deacons. Our biggest role was caring for the senior adult members of our church. We had about two thousand members, and about half or more of them were over sixty-five. Many of those were in their eighties and confined to nursing or care homes. One of my duties as Deacon was to visit those people and serve them communion on the days our church had communion services. I discovered that serving this community of aged people was more joy to me than perhaps the joy I brought to them. It became my calling.

Living in Leisure World was wonderful – two large swimming pools, two 18-hole golf courses, 20+ miles of streets to walk, a fitness center that was the biggest and best equipment of anything west of the Mississippi. Several of the wealthier residents had pitched in to fund its construction. The fitness center, built beside the pool, had a spa and every kind of exercise equipment you could hope to find. When it was too hot to walk (which was a major part of the year), I spent a lot of time at this center.

While living here, I became president of the computer club and one of the first founders of the writers club, later becoming its second president.

I had bought an older house and later put about $40,000 in upgrades into it. When I had to sell in 2009, the market had crashed, and I lost all that money. I got my equity out of the house, but not the money I spent on upgrades. I listed the house in October 2008, and it was April 2009 before it finally sold. I was lucky. So many homes just like mine (the same model) continued to sit, reclaimed by the bank, or foreclosed, sad and forlorn looking. The housing market was pretty ugly, so I was lucky to sell my house.

Tommy

Tommy, my oldest son, died February 10, 2007 of Melanoma. Doctors removed a huge Melanoma from his back in the early 90s. Several years later a tumor was removed from under his shoulder blade, and all the lymph nodes on that side found to contain Melanoma. Shortly after that, he had tumors in his brain.

One special trip I made in the summer of 2007, after Tom died, was to visit Di (Tommy's widow) at her home in Meadview, the place that she and Tommy had built. Not far away was the Hualapai Indian tribe who lived at the bottom of the Grand Canyon.

The tribe was trying desperately to become self-sufficient and raise themselves out of poverty. With the help of a developer, they had built the "Skywalk," which was a horseshoe-shaped glass-bottomed walkway, which projected out several feet from the sheer cliffs of the Grand Canyon. The actual area was called "Grand Canyon West" and was west of the Grand Canyon proper – the famous site visited by millions of tourists yearly. Diana and another friend, Lynn, and I walked the Skywalk. I get terrible vertigo from heights, so this was not one of my favorite trips, the Skywalk being 4000 feet above the canyon floor. At the end of the trip, photographers took our pictures to prove we had been there. At the end of our skywalk, we were on a tour that gave us a meal at one of the stops along the canyon top.

Information about Grand Canyon West and its attractions are at http://www.grandcanyonwest.com/the-grand-canyon-skywalk/

Tom died on February 10, 2007 and was buried on the 16th. His service had more people than the preacher had ever seen at a funeral. Friends, relatives from around the country, long-time buddies around Mesa, and his work partners attended. The owners of the business where he worked shut down for the day so everyone could attend the service. I was stunned to see so many people. The service and burial took place at Mountainview Cemetery in east Mesa. It is a beautiful, well-maintained place with its own crematorium. I cried for two years.

Since son Tom had died in 2007, his wife remarried in 2009 and his sons were scattered, two of them in Iraq and Afghanistan. My daughter, Tracy and her husband, Don, wanted me to come to Grover Beach, California, to live near them.

I really miss Arizona, having lived there for four decades, and seeing almost every corner of the state. There is very little I haven't seen. The North

Rim of the Grand Canyon is far more spectacular than the South Rim. The Sky Islands – (Mt. Graham, Mt. Lemmon, the San Francisco Peaks, the Mogollon (pronounced "mo-gi-Yon") peaks, Kitt Peak National Observatory, the Huachuca mountains) are fascinating. You will drive from desert landscape to the top of the mountain where there are tall pines and ski resorts. Along the way the drive goes through five climatic zones. We used to go camping in the Huachucas. At night, being far above civilization, we could see every star in the sky. It was mind-boggling.

I moved to Grover Beach with Tracy and Don in April 2009, spending a month with them. In looking for an apartment, few would rent to someone with a dog. Consequently, I ended up finding an apartment in Santa Maria. It was a nice apartment complex, professionally run and well maintained, but in an area infested with gangs, making it dangerous to go out at night. I lived there for nine months until an apartment became available for me at Cortina d'Arroyo Grande in Arroyo Grande, California in January 2010.

Family Reunions

When most people have family reunions, they gather at grandma's house or a local park. There may be treats and rides for the children. The big events are Barbeques, with roast corn, hot dogs, and potato salad. People would be sitting about in their best informal garb, their feet up, the dogs running around, and if it's raining they just go inside. Homemade ice cream is often a big treat.

However, when we Eisenhowers have a reunion, it's a matter of public record and all the stops are pulled out to make it a grand affair. Schedules for each day's events are handed out, and reservations are made for each day's luncheons and dinners. Reporters and photographers show up, and many of the activities are reported in the local newspapers and often in the national news. There is not much time or place for any of us to be informal, except in the privacy of our motel rooms. We must be careful not to be photographed smoking cigarettes or with an alcoholic drink in hand. We all must be very circumspect. Many dignitaries were always around. They were wonderful affairs, but far from casual.

We usually stayed at a local motel, and once the Holiday Inn Express in Abilene was built right off I-70, we stayed there. There was much more room and great amenities for the crowd of people we were.

When the reporters and photographers showed up, my cousins and I often would hide in the restrooms. However, my brother, Earl Eisenhower, Jr. and my cousin, Milton Eisenhower, Jr., would step up and face the mob of journalists. I was happy to see them do that.

Always, the family reunions would celebrate, or commemorate, a special event in the lives of the Eisenhowers.

Family Reunions 1987, 1990, 1994, 2010

Reunion 1987 – 100th Anniversary of the Eisenhower Home and 25th Anniversary of the Dedication of the Library

The planning usually began with a letter from the Director, Dwight D. Eisenhower Library, giving us family members a heads up as to what activities were planned. The first event would be a dinner on the first evening of our arrival and lunch and dinner the next day hosted by the Eisenhower Foundation.

We had to fill out special forms regarding transportation, time of arrival and other details. The Eisenhower Foundation would then reserve rooms for all the family members at Priem's Pride Motel. At the first reunion in 1987 we had only 14 members (of the third generation of the family) scheduled to arrive.

There were special programs and lectures given by the Eisenhower Library in the Auditorium of the Visitors Center.

Pictures were taken. John, Dwight's son, and Peggy Bryan (Roy Eisenhower's daughter) were the only ones missing of our generation of the family in 1987.

It was always great to get together with all our cousins because we all lived so far apart, and reunions were few and far between. The previous reunion was in 1945 when we all celebrated Uncle Ike's homecoming in Abilene.

This reunion was pretty simple compared to future reunions.

Permission granted by Eisenhower Presidential Library & Museum originator of the photo.

1987 Reunion picture, the direct descendants of five of the six Eisenhower brothers:

Barry Eisenhower (son of Earl Jr.); Earl Jr.; Susan & William Eisenhower Causin (grandson of Ed); Sally & Milton S. Eisenhower Jr.; Bruce & Jean Causin Ramey (she is granddaughter of Ed); Kaye Eisenhower Morgan; Janis Eisenhower

& William O. Causin (she is Ed's daughter); Mary Jean Eisenhower & Clifton (she is Dwight's granddaughter)

100th Anniversary of Dwight Eisenhower's Birth 1990

This reunion was a blast – the celebration to end all celebrations. A real blowout! Cousin Bud (Milton Jr.) helped to orchestrate this event, with all the family staying, once again, at Priem's Pride Motel in Abilene. The celebrations would take place from Thursday, October 11, 1990 through Sunday, October 14, 1990, with all of us planning on leaving Monday October 15. The staff carefully orchestrated events, planned to the nth degree. All family members had to acknowledge that they would be attending, in order to have the proper tickets for admission and seating for the various events.

The Eisenhower Library people quickly got involved in planning all the various ceremonies, luncheons, concerts, dances and honor ceremonies, with Cousin Bud communicating with them, then forwarding information to the rest of us.

The event planned for October 11 was a family gathering in the hospitality suite of the motel.

On Friday, the 12th, the plans were for all the family to visit the Eisenhower Center, the Museum, and the Library. We would split up so groups would not be clogging up the areas. In the evening, the family (only) were guests of the Eisenhower Foundation at the Abilene Country Club. Following dinner, a canteen dance (informal, of course) was held at the local high school, like the old sock hops of past years. We were encouraged to wear saddle shoes and bobby socks.

Some of us also had to take time to visit the old home. I always loved being there, among Grandma Ida's favorite flowers. Once sun-reflective screening was put on the windows to preserve the furniture, the original flowers died, and artificial ones substituted. The old Bible and their original furniture are intact from 150 years ago. I have visited the home many times, having driven out to Abilene in the 1950s when Tom and I were living in Kansas City. The baby picture on the landing on the stairwell was of me when I was about six months old. We family members were allowed to go upstairs to see the old rooms. Sadly, there wasn't much to see, as everything is covered in white sheets. At least my kids could see the rooms and how much (or how little furniture) was in the rooms. There were no real closets, just indentations in the wall to hang clothes, and a bureau to put folded clothes. The proverbial chamber pots were there, too.

We were also informed that an Eisenhower family photograph would be taken at 5 pm on the front porch of the Eisenhower Boyhood Home.

On Saturday, the 13th we attended a first-day issue ceremony of an Eisenhower Commemorative stamp at the Eisenhower Library. Following the stamp commemoration a luncheon was held in the courtyard of the library. Later that afternoon we got to see the Eisenhower staff train, the relic from the 1950s. Again, dinner was planned, and family gathered in the hospitality suite. There was also a special gala at the Expocenter in Topeka, at which John (Dwight's son) spoke.

There was a special luncheon held on the 13th, by invitation only and in the evening, a private premiere of a new movie about Dwight D. Eisenhower.

All of the above events mentioned were by invitation only and we family members had to submit reservations that we would be there. Some events had a small fee; others were free to family members.

On Sunday, October 14,, the date of Dwight Eisenhower's birthday, the non-denominational memorial church service was held on the grounds of the Center, with about twenty thousand people attending. Dignitaries present were Colin Powell, Billy Graham (who was Uncle Ike's favorite preacher) who gave a scriptural lesson, and several others.

Other events included a Dedication of a Memorial Tree by the Kansas Association of Garden Clubs. Following that was a wreath-laying ceremony and Military Honor Guard at Uncle Ike's Grave site. Uncle Ike and Aunt Mamie are buried in the Chapel of Meditation on the grounds of the Center. Their first son, Doud Dwight, who died of Scarlet Fever at age three at Camp Meade, Maryland is buried with them.

A luncheon followed the above-listed events, hosted by the Eisenhower Library. At 1:30 pm the U.S. Army Band Concert presented a concert at the Eisenhower Center. At 3:00 pm the WWII air show was held at the Abilene Airport. At 4:30 pm a canteen dance with vintage entertainment and military band was held at the fairgrounds.

At 6:30 pm on Sunday the fireworks display was held at the Eisenhower Center with 20,000 people in attendance. The total population of Abilene at the time was about 10,000, and I couldn't imagine that many people on the grounds of the center, but they were counted.

The last event of the weekend was, of course, gathering in the hospitality suite. What a grand time we had. That would be the last time I would see four of my cousins, three of whom died a few years later, including Johnny, who died in December 2013. My brother Bud (Earl Jr.) died in September 2012, age 76. I still miss him.

The best event of the Sunday gathering was the luncheon aboard a pair of Burlington Northern dining cars. The railroad siding was very near, almost beside the Eisenhower Boyhood Home. All kinds of dignitaries were there, and in the private, informal setting of the luxurious dining aboard, we had a chance to meet and greet some of the dignitaries. Son-in-Law Don Groshong was so excited to meet Billy Graham, and had his picture taken with him.

On Sunday the 14th, the 100th anniversary of Dwight Eisenhower's birth, all kinds of special events and ceremonies were held. There were many illustrious people there also: Richard Norton Smith, Acting Director of the Eisenhower Library who went on to the Hoover Library and eventually the Nixon Library; Billy Graham (who gave a stirring speech for 20,000 people on Sunday morning); Richard Halverson, Chaplain of the United States Senate (he helped to coordinate with every church in Abilene), who conducted the worship service; a 170-voice choir assembled for the occasion; Senator Bob Dole and Nancy Landon Kassebaum; Rep. Pat Roberts; Winston Churchill II; President Bush's representative; General Colin L. Powell, Chairman, Joint Chiefs of Staff, who was the last speaker before the wreath laying ceremony. The First Infantry Division Band from Fort Riley performed "Soldier of Democracy." The Wreath-laying at the Chapel of Meditation took place directly following the band presentation.

After the morning religious services, at noon, the Columbine II flew over the Eisenhower Center – it made several passes. The Columbine II is a historic plane, the second of three "Columbines" that Uncle Ike used. A consortium of four people bought Columbine II hopes of restoring it. They bought the plane in the hopes of refurbishing it and selling or presenting it to the Eisenhower Center. They got the plane working, it could fly, but the guts had nothing left. A former White House staffer, who had flown many times in the Columbine II was working with this group to finalize the needs to refurbish the insides. The cost was mighty! Unfortunately, this group was never able to obtain the financing needed. The Eisenhower Center would not take it, saying they did not have the budget or finances to afford upkeep and insurance. The plane sits today, sad and broken, in a boneyard in Marana, Arizona.

> *As an addendum, the following information came to me May 2, 2015: Subject: Columbine II will fly again*
>
> *Columbine II, the first presidential a/c to be called Air Force One, will be under new ownership this summer as a restoration process gets under way in Arizona. Dynamic Aviation of Bridgewater, Virginia completed its due diligence this week and decided to proceed with the purchase of the 1948 Lockheed C-121A Constellation (48-0610) used by President Dwight D. Eisenhower. Owners Harry Oliver and Lockie Christler - son of the late Mel Christler, who had owned it for years - will sell the Connie to Dynamic founder Karl. D. Stoltzfus Sr. "After extensive inspection and repairs on the aircraft we are ready to accept it, and to proceed with closing in June. Many challenges remain before we can fly it to Virginia but we are now confident that it is feasible,"*

> *Stoltzfus credits the present owners for hanging on to Columbine II through the years and investing in its preservation. "Without their dedication and their efforts to preserve it, it would most likely have been melted down long ago," he said. Among the project's other supporters are Mid America Flight Museum of Mt. Pleasant, Texas. The Air Force retired Columbine II in 1968 and sold it as surplus in 1970. It then sat in salvage yards in Arizona until 1990 when it was made airworthy again, then after a flying a few hours it was parked in Marana in 2003 and hasn't moved since. Dynamic wants to make the aircraft airworthy and fly it home as a certificated aircraft rather than on a ferry permit; no completion date has been set.*

We family members got to go through the Columbine II. Memorable! Columbine I was the plane Uncle Ike used in WWII; Columbine III is the plane he used from 1954 to 1961 and is currently at the Dayton Museum.

The final event Sunday evening, the 14th, was the fireworks display. Never have I seen such an all-out unlimited sky-is-the-limit fireworks. The sky was one big cloud of smoke after setting off many fireworks during the hour-long show. The final display was a laser projection of an image of Uncle Ike on the clouds as a backdrop. It was spectacular! There was a recording playing. It was eerie as if Uncle Ike himself was overseeing the events.

Seating for all events was limited – we had to make sure we communicated with the Eisenhower Center that we planned to be there.

This particular event was the most splendiferous event ever staged by the Eisenhower Center. It was billed as the biggest fireworks and laser show in Kansas history. It must have cost a fortune. Events like this typically have donors who give huge amounts to allay costs, but I'm sure the Center will never have such an event as this until 2090, on Dwight Eisenhower's 200th birthday! There were 20,000 people on the campus that evening!

Such is the Eisenhower Family Reunions! Coordinated, planned, orchestrated, structured, but still fun. We had to make our own fun amidst all the furor of such a structured event.

Eisenhower Family Reunion 1990
Permission granted by Eisenhower Presidential Library & Museum the originator of the photo.

Pictured here are:

Front row – Ralph & Mary Jean Eisenhower Atwater (she is Dwight's granddaughter); Jennifer Eisenhower (daughter of Milton Jr. "Bud"); Peg (daughter of Roy Eisenhower) & Jack Bryan; Mrs. Bob (Evelyn) Fegan (granddaughter of Roy Eisenhower) and son Brad Fegan, Bob Fegan; Earl Eisenhower Jr.

Back row – Susan & Bill Causin (grandson of Ed Eisenhower, son of Janis & Bill Causin);

Sally & Milton S. (Bud) Eisenhower, Jr.; Janis & Bill Causin; Kaye Eisenhower Morgan (daughter of Earl Sr.); Tracy (daughter of Kaye Morgan) & Don Groshong; Lois & Michael Fegan (grandson of Roy); John and Joanne Eisenhower; Jeanne Causin Ramey (granddaughter of Ed); Edgar Eisenhower Causin (son of William Causin Jr., grandson of Ed Eisenhower).

Children sitting on the right: Michael Eisenhower Ramey and Kirsten Causin (KC) Ramey (children of Jeanne & Bruce Ramey); and Lynn Causin

This is Columbine II parked at the Abilene Airport. We were able to go through it. It is now in a boneyard in Marana, Arizona. This plane was flown over the Sunday noon services being held on the grounds of the Eisenhower Compound.

50th Anniversary of Normandy Reunion 1994

This reunion was May 11th through the 15th, held a few weeks earlier than the actual D-Day celebration. The Eisenhower Library and Museum staff people were planning on going to Normandy for the annual reunion/celebration there, but this year would be special for them

First on our agendas would be visits to the Family Home, Library, Museum, and Visitor Center, as usual, with a reception held later that first evening.

The next day there were panel discussions in the morning and evening, with lunch on our own, and later that evening a reception and formal dinner in the Library Courtyard. Bagpiper Bill Millin supplied entertainment.

The third day was a special wreath-laying ceremony at the Chapel of Meditation, with cousin Bud (Milton, Jr.) representing the family in laying the wreath. After the wreath-laying, the 1st Infantry Division Band from Ft. Riley, Kansas performed. Presentations and discussions followed, with lunch in the Library Courtyard for dignitaries and family.

At the end of the third day was an excursion to the various cemeteries by Tom Branigar, Library

Archivist. This was an awesome trip to see where so many of my ancestors are buried. I love to tramp old cemeteries, having been a genealogy researcher for several years. Cemeteries are full of history, recorded on gravestones. Tom Branigar, as the Archivist in charge of Eisenhower history, would be helpful to me in later years when I was researching and writing The Eisenhower Legacy, a Tribute to Ida Stover and David Jacob Eisenhower.

In tramping through these several cemeteries, I noticed that there were many small headstones for children's burials. Most of them were deaths due to smallpox. I was stunned to see so many children's graves. It must have been extremely sad for families who lost these children.

At the end of this third day, we family members had a private dinner at Victorian Reflections. This is a wonderful old Victorian mansion, converted to a restaurant and Bed & Breakfast. Lots of history here, and the former home of Swede Hazlett, Dwight's best friend, before they both left for West Point.

Again, a highly structured time, but thoroughly enjoyable, and great to see my cousins and have Don and Tracy and their girls with us.

With events like these, we always come home with tons of pictures.

Another thing I came across is a list of all the divisions, units, troops, brigades, armored divisions, companies, etc. that took part in the D-Day invasion from June 6 to August 31, 1944. The list has all the landing sites and details of which country's ships will be landing and where. Also on this list is a total listing by name of all the ships: Battleships, Cruisers, Destroyers, Frigates, Corvettes, Minesweepers, Patrol Craft and other ships, including all the British, French and American ships. Fascinating, especially for anyone interested in military warfare history.

Publishing My Book
May 1, 2010

After years of research and writing, editing and re-editing, my first book was finally ready for publishing. My brother, Earl, agreed to foot the bill for initial publishing. Roesler Enterprises Publishing, 1154 E. Kramer Circle, Mesa, Arizona, 85203 were the publishers who arranged the book's release on May 1, 2010, the anniversary of my grandmother Ida's birth.

The book was about the life of Ida and David Eisenhower, parents of six boys who all grew up to be the best in their chosen profession. How they attained such high positions in spite of their poor background living in Abilene, Kansas is a story for the ages. Another reason for my writing the book was that many myths and untruths abounded about the family's early history, their lives and living in Abilene. I just had to set the record straight.

The Roselers arranged for a shipment of books to the Abilene Visitors Center, and we worked with the Library personnel to accommodate the release, publication and celebration of the book.

When my brother and I arrived in Abilene, some of my cousins were already there – my cousin Pat's children and their families. It was good to see them. Lots of local press people were there also, and once again we were headline news for a day or so.

Earl and I helped to plant the first vegetables in the Victory Garden though the soil was so wet after heavy rains the previous days; I doubted that these vegetables would survive.

Karl Weissenbach, Earl Eisenhower, Jr. & Kaye Eisenhower Morgan after planting our Victory Garden. Karl is Director of the Eisenhower Library and Museum

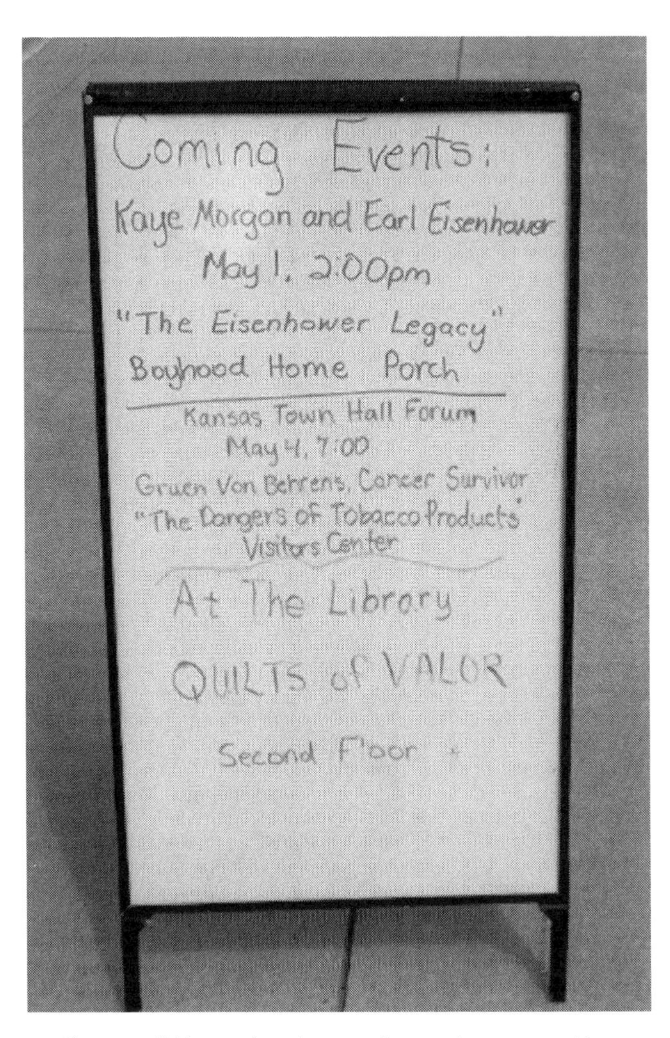

One of the signboards set up on the Eisenhower Center campus advertising the talk Earl Eisenhower and Kaye Eisenhower Morgan would be giving on the front porch of the Boyhood Home

Earl and I on the front porch of our grandparents' home preparing setup for the talk we would give, and the crowd on the front lawn during our talk

We had an official book signing at the Visitor Center and sales of the book were doing well that day.

Eventually, the Eisenhower Library included my book on the Library's official list of reference books. What an honor.

During the period of research, I made many trips and spent a lot of time in Abilene, talking with people who remembered my grandparents, and people who had worked with Grandfather David. I talked many times with Charles Stover, a nephew of Ida, who had apple and potato farms near Topeka and used to visit Ida and David often when he came to Abilene to sell his produce. I was very fortunate to meet and visit and talk with all these people because a few short years later, all of them were gone. Nevertheless they all helped to fill in a lot of blanks in my family history.

Also important was my correspondence with cousin John, Dwight's son. We had always been fairly close though communication was sparse at times. Since Johnny had spent summers with Grandpa David and Grandmother Ida when he was young, he was an excellent resource. He also had been in Abilene in 1938 when our family was visiting David and Ida. We had much email communication back and forth for two or three years, and he was an immense help to me.

One time, a few years ago, I spent three weeks in Abilene. Usually, I would drive to Abilene by myself, thereby having the freedom to come and go as I wished. I spent the entire three weeks, every day from 9:00 am to 5:00 pm, at the Eisenhower Library combing through every scrap of evidence, writings, records and details I could find. Archivist Thomas Branigar was of immense help to me. He always knew where to find exactly what I wanted. I could not have completed all the work I did on my first book without his help.

I also got to know various residents of Abilene, some of whom remembered the Creamery where David had worked, others who remembered Ida and her supporting the River Brethren Church. One lead would lead to another. It's amazing how a chain of events or people can lead one on to further information.

I learned the truth about the location of David and Ida's marriage, where they were married and why. The myth that they were married in the chapel of the university at Lecompton was not true. They were actually married at her brother's (Rev. William D. Stover) home in Lecompton by the Reverend E. B. Slade of the United Brethren in Christ Church of Lecompton. The Brethren in

Christ Church was one of many River Brethren churches in Kansas at that time. About 20 people attended the ceremony, which was written up in the Lecompton news the next day.

One funny incident of that trip was when Dan Holt and his wife, Marilyn, invited me to dinner. They have a lovely old Victorian home on the main street in Abilene. One of the things my mother always taught me was that when you are invited to dinner on an occasion such as this, you take candy, flowers or wine for the hostess. I ruled out candy and considered a bottle of fine wine. Not being a connoisseur of wine, I ruled that out and decided to get a nice bouquet of flowers. A good thing! When I arrived at the Holt's home, I learned that Dan was a wine aficionado and had basement shelves full of fine wines. He also was a gourmet cook. He had a chef's gourmet kitchen in the remodeled house. The dinner was beyond excellence. Different wines were served with the appetizer course, salad, main meal and for dessert. Dan looked at Marilyn at the end of the meal and said, "Shall we break out the good stuff?" They did so. Dan went down into the cellar and brought out a magnum of wine for our dessert course. He explained that this wine was given him by the French at a previous Normandy D-Day

Commemoration. What luck! The dinner and wine were fantastic! Thank you, Dan and Marilyn.

While in Abilene I was able to meet and have lunch with other friends whom I had met over the years. It was great to see them.

Trips to Germany, Washington, D.C. and Gettysburg 1990s – 2000s

Germany – 1993 and 2000

Twice I spent three weeks in Germany with my German friends and their families. Both are teachers at the grade school level, retired now. The first time I visited was in 1993, and it was good to see my friends again. I had first met them in 1969 when they were with a group of students from Germany who stayed with our church members that summer. I visited them the second time in 2000.

When I arrived in Bitz, the small village in southwestern Germany where Heide and Hilger and their three children lived, I was greeted warmly with welcoming signs, the whole works.

Bitz was a delightful village and very typical of other villages around Germany, part ancient and part modern. Their way of life and building codes were so different from what we as Americans experience. Ancient buildings are preserved and rebuilt in the old mode to preserve their culture and history.

Before leaving for my first trip to Germany, I took two semesters of German from a German lady at the local community college. We learned not only the language, but also culture and habits. It was eye-opening and well worth my time. During my time in Germany, I was dreaming in German and could converse well enough with family and shopkeepers. In approaching a shopkeeper, I would ask, "Sprechen sie English?"

Usually, they would say, "Nein." I could then talk easily (or fairly so) with them in German. My friends told me that speaking the native language was greatly appreciated.

I heard many stories of American tourists who traveled to Germany and tried to demand services in English, and consequently were ignored. The Americans then thought the Germans to be very rude. On my second trip in 2000, a friend and I were in a restaurant where the waitresses spoke only German. My friend thought everyone should understand English, but I talked with the waitress in German and was able to order what we wanted. My friend walked out of the restaurant in a huff because the waitresses did not speak English;

I ordered for her, but she still wasn't satisfied. Consequently, when she walked out, she left me stuck with the bill and refused to repay me.

I could truly write a book about my trips to Germany, but what impressed me most was the ancient culture and the history of Germany. My Father's ancestry was pure German on both the paternal and maternal side of his parentage. The Eisenhower name and history did not escape me even on this trip. Dad's history was southern Germany. Mother's history was northern and eastern Germany and Scotland. So, Germany meant a lot to me, especially since doing so much genealogical research. Dad's ancestors moved from Germany, into Switzerland, then to France, then to America. Tracing them is another story in itself.

The other thing that impressed me was the fact that Uncle Ike was the commander who headed up Germany's defeat. When he and his troops accomplished the defeat of Germany, Uncle Ike shed tears, thinking that all his family was from Germany. It pained him terribly to see Germany so decimated.

My friend, Heide, was anxious to have me meet an elderly man in her neighborhood who had been a soldier in World War II. We finally met outside one day, and she introduced me to him, explaining with much pride that I was the niece of General Eisenhower. The Eisenhower name never escapes me. This old man – he must have been about 80 – came up to me, face to face, stuck his finger in my face and said, "Let me tell YOU about the war!" Being the old German that he was, speaking in German, he let me have it, describing in detail what his war years were like. It wasn't fun for him or his fellow soldiers, probably worse, or possibly much worse than what our soldiers fared. So much for trying to impress a former German soldier with the Eisenhower name! It didn't go far, but I could understand Heide's trying, and I could understand the old man's pride in his heritage and the pain he suffered for many years.

What blew me away was being submersed in the culture, being away from the tourist crowd, I got to experience what being German is all about. It suddenly dawned on me that this was what my father was like. I finally began to understand him better than I ever had before. He had the discipline, the steadfast love, the cultural habits, the sense of humor and being strong when others weren't, the push for education, both secular and religious. Education was extremely important, as it was for the Germans, who believed in a strong mind, soul and body. Both his maternal and paternal ancestors were all German, and that probably explains his habits and mannerisms from his heritage and the culture.

When Hilger would call one of the children, they would stand up immediately and answer, "Yes, Papa!" Boy, that I could have such obedience from my children! But all of their three children turned out to be great people, graduating from Universities and doing well in the world.

When I first arrived at their home, Hilger sat down with me and a map of Germany. He asked, "Kaye, where would you like to go?" I named several small towns where ancestors had lived. He looked them up on the map and declared that we could indeed see these towns. All were in southern Germany and not far away.

Tubingen was one of the small towns I was interested in – an ancestor of mine had been the Wine Master at Tubingen University in the early 18th century. We got to visit that town near where Hilger's brother and his wife live, and the University.

Many of the smaller towns in Germany were left relatively untouched by the War, so I got to see the actual homes where my ancestors had lived. In some cases, I could not identify the actual house, but the neighborhood. The architecture of the homes defines the century they were built, so it was easy to see which neighborhoods were built in the 17th, 18th and 19th centuries.

In another case, my Matter (mah-ter) ancestors came from a tiny village called Alteckendorf in the northern part of Alsace-Lorraine. We traveled over there, through the Black Forest, through Strasburg where the great cathedral is. We stopped to visit the cathedral in Strasburg. The cathedral is the center of the religious order in this part of France. More information of its history can be found at http://www.strasbourg.info/cathedral/, and http://www.frenchmoments.eu/strasbourg-cathedral/. Strasbourg Cathedral is a most fantastic place to see. So much history.

In history, Alsace-Lorraine was German, then French, then German again, and finally French as the Germans and French finally made a treaty that extended France's borders to the Rhine River. As we arrived in the tiny village of ancient homes, there was a man on the sidewalk. I asked Hilger to stop the car. I got out, approached the man and asked him (in German, of course) if he knew any Matters. He replied, in a dialect Heide and I found hard to follow, "Ah, Matter, he is coming to pick me up!" I told him to say "hello" to Herr Matter from his American cousin. (Rebecca Matter was the mother of my grandfather David Eisenhower. Johannes Matter, born in Alteckendorf, participated in the

Revolutionary War, was the great grandfather of Rebecca Matter).

One of the things we try to do in researching ancestors is to find the ancient churches and graveyards. We found the parsonage and the graveyard. Approaching the Parsonage, we found the pastor's wife at home, but the pastor was not. She invited us in and sat us on the back patio and fed us tea and cookies. She explained that her husband had gone to Strasburg on important church business. Telling her what we were looking for, she brought out record books dating back to 1800, explaining that the ledgers should have been put in the archives in Strasburg many years ago. I'm so glad the ledgers were still there. My direct ancestors had all left the area by about 1750, but all these people, the Matters, covered the pages of the ledger she showed us – were collateral ancestors.

Next, we visited the church graveyard. In Germany, as in much of Europe, the first burial is very deep. After twenty years, the family is allowed to sell the gravesite. They remove the original gravestone, and the next person is buried on top of the first one. So it goes through the decades. We had no way of knowing how many were buried in this graveyard. However, many of the names on the tombstones were Matters. Even the wives' maiden names were shown, which is rare. There were Matters everywhere. What an experience! My great grandmother's ancestors, and here was history in reality!

The interesting thing I noted about Alteckendorf was the mixture of French and German, the land having been conquered back and forth over the centuries by France and Germany. It is now France, within the district of Alsace-Lorraine. In walking the streets, I noted homes that were very scruffy, overgrown, in need of maintenance or repair. Invariably these were French, noting their names on mailboxes. Other homes were neat, tidy, beautiful flower gardens and homes in pristine condition. I noted the German names on their mailboxes. A strange country. Heide said the French need to be more like Germans, and Germans need to be more like French.

Street scene in old part of Alteckendorf.
Note the large gates facing the streets,
installed to prevent the tax collector from
seeing any household equipment.

On to Grossgartach where my Link ancestors lived. The Links in America claim ancestry to Dwight David Eisenhower, as well they should. Ida Stover Eisenhower's mother was a Link. At the time she was growing up in Virginia there were Links everywhere. The name Link figures prominently in family records of births, deaths, wills and property transactions. A Link collateral ancestor was the inventor of the Link Trainer, used widely in World War II to train pilots. It was Ida's Link grandfather who provided, in his will, the inheritance that Ida and her brothers received. The inheritance enabled all of them to move west from war-torn Virginia.

The Links who came to this country, my direct ancestors, left Grossgartach, Germany, sometime in the early 1700s.

Hilger and I located where Grossgartach should be on the map, but when we drove over there, we had a hard time finding it. (We learned eventually that Grossgartach, the old town, was smack in the middle of the new town, Leingarten – no wonder we couldn't find it) Finally, we decided to stop and ask directions. Seeing a farmer near his farmhouse, we stopped to ask him directions. In the process of talking with him, the farmer's ancient mother, Frau Zaiser, who must have been 90, came out on the balcony, wildly gesticulating that we must "come up, come up." Well, we couldn't refuse such a grand gesture, so we all (there were four of us) trundled up the stairs to the second-floor kitchen.

The lady, as I mentioned, must have been about 90, tiny, wispy little thing and as spry as a spring chicken. She and her only remaining son ran the large farm that their house overlooked. This old lady had been run over by a tractor on their farm a couple years or so before this and was in the hospital for several months, but miraculously survived.

The kitchen was about 30 or 40 feet long, with a balcony overlooking their farmland. The flooring was linoleum, and a trestle table was against one wall with parson bench seating against the wall. Facing seating was a long backless bench. Appliances were an electric stove and small refrigerator. Homes in Germany did not, as a rule, have large refrigerators as we do in America.

The view from the kitchen balcony showed a wide expanse of green, fertile land stretching for many acres. Frau Zaiser and her son farmed this land by themselves.

Frau Zaiser sat us down at the table, and asked what kind of wine we would like – red wine or white wine? We all told her our preferences (red wine), and grabbing a glass pitcher from the kitchen, she scooted down the hallway and was back in a jiffy with a pitcher full of red wine. She poured wine into each of our glasses, which were ordinary water glasses. The glasses were full to the brim. I thought, "I guess this is how Germans drink their wine," and didn't give it much thought. However, in Germany, it is polite to always finish everything the hostess puts in front of you, so I knew I'd have to drink the full glass.

When I finally was able to finish the glass of wine, I was shocked to turn back and find that she had filled my glass again. Wow! Hilger helped me finish it. He had been drinking lemonade with his wine, which is common for the designated driver.

In talking with this lady and telling her what we were looking for, she explained that Grossgartach – the old city – was now surrounded by the newer town of Leingarten. She also talked of the Links and told us that she was a small girl when the last Link left Grossgartach around 1910. She told us where to find my ancestor's house. He had been a blacksmith, as had his descendants who continued to live in the old home and follow the trade that had been handed down through the generations.

We found the old home, and I've got pictures of it. It still has some of the blacksmithing equipment beside the house, behind the tall, wooden gates.

The Link home in Grossgartach, Germany, where my ancestors had lived. Some of the blacksmithing equipment is still there, in the back. Homes of that age were built with massive gates fronting on the street so the tax collector could not see anything on their property.

Later, in Leingarten, we found the museum where some Link blacksmithing equipment now resides, along with the family's other household items. The Germans take great pride in presenting to the public the knowledge of the Link ancestry to President Eisenhower.

One of the first women, who married a Link and migrated to this country, was born in Bieberach (which means "beaver"). We found the street of homes where she most likely lived. There are several Bieberachs in Germany – about five if I remember – so it is important to know the district (much like our counties or states) where a certain town might be located.

On to Dachau – visiting this prison camp was a horrifying experience. I refused to go near the crematories. The museum within the confines of the prison grounds was very interesting. Everything was done in black, gray and white, to convey the message of death that was here. It was very somber.

Dachau was one of the camps General Eisenhower toured, took many pictures, then forced the local villagers to come into the camps and clean them up. The pictures were graphic proof of what the Nazis had done to exterminate the Jews. The General said he wanted the world to see this devastation, so the world would never forget.

He said, "Sometime in the future, (someone) will come along and claim this never happened!"

I asked Germans I met what they knew of the death camps. Apparently, the ones who had lived in the small villages had no knowledge. That's what they told me. Heide's parents' home was devastated during the war and they had no money to rebuild. They had to rebuild, a stone and brick at a time. It took them years.

When I tried to talk with Heide's mother, she did not understand me well, and I found it hard to understand her also. Heide then explained that most older folks spoke "common or Vulgate" German, and did not understand the "learned" German that people like me get from textbooks. Also – there are many dialects throughout Germany, and many Germans find it hard to communicate with each other because of that. The German spoken in Alsace-Lorraine is the same German dialect that the Amish and Mennonite in the United States speak to this day. It is a different dialect and the reason Heide and I found it hard to speak with the man we met on the street in Alteckendorf.

During my trips to Germany, we also visited Bavaria (Munich-"Munchen") and the Hofbrau House and the ancient cathedral and town square. In Austria and Switzerland, we found many sights to see. We stayed overnight in gasthoffs where the morning breakfasts are truly filling. We saw Berchtesgaden where Hitler built his Eagles Aerie on top of the mountain. We then went on to Salzburg, Austria where we saw an ancient cathedral, the old "Salt Castle," (Salzburg) and Mozart's birthplace. We went to Switzerland a couple of times, once to buy groceries, cheaper than in Germany, in a little town on Lake Constance. Another time we took the bus to Zurich. We went by train to Augsburg, a very ancient city that celebrated its 1000th year when Christ was born. A fascinating place.

We also visited many other ancient cathedrals, monasteries and sites of great interest.

Gettysburg
1953, 1992 and 2004

I have been fortunate to visit Gettysburg, Uncle Ike and Aunt Mamie's first "permanent" home.

The first time we saw the property was right after Ike and Mamie had bought the place, in 1953. We visited when my chaperones and I were traveling from Penn State to Winchester, Virginia, for the Apple Blossom Festival. When we came to the main house, the caretaker told us that his children had measles, and it was not wise to tour the property at the time.

The Eisenhower's Gettysburg property was private land within the confines of the Gettysburg National Military Park. Another man owned adjoining land, and he used to join with Uncle Ike in marketing their Black Angus cattle. When they showed their cattle at auctions and cattle shows, fictitious names were used to prevent bias in the judging. They garnered several blue ribbons.

Uncle Ike's will stated that Mamie should continue to live there after his death. He stipulated that the land after her death would be turned over to the Gettysburg National Military Park, and become a part of the Park.

The second time I went to Gettysburg, in 1992, I talked with the Rangers there and arranged a private tour of Uncle Ike's property. Because I was an Eisenhower, I was able to access parts of the house and property that regular tourists cannot go. I was able to go upstairs to the bedroom areas, and outside to the various barns. None of the barns were available to the public at the time. From the top of the hill on the farm, overlooking one of the main roads entering Gettysburg, we could look down on a site that was slated to become a fast food restaurant. Apparently the local people brought together enough money to buy the land and keep it from being developed, thereby protecting the view that you would see from the farm.

I arranged a special tour with a tour driver. The tour drivers, or Park Docents and Rangers, drive your car throughout the Battlefield and Gettysburg. During the drive, they give you a running commentary. I was able to view all the sites unimpeded since I was a passenger. Having the Ranger or Docent drive your car is a fantastic way to view the Battlefield and tour Gettysburg. It is wonderful to talk and spend time with these tour drivers. They know so much about the battle of Gettysburg and the town of Gettysburg. They are very interesting people. My hat is off to them. They do a great job!

After staying in Gettysburg and touring the battlefield and the town, I realized that the whole town is hallowed ground. Musket balls exist everywhere, permanently embedded in walls of homes.

The last time I visited Gettysburg in 2004, again I arranged with the Rangers for special tours. With me were my friends Joan and George from Kensington, Maryland, with whom I was staying during my brief visit East. We got to see much of what I had seen on my 1993 trip, including the barns and the upstairs. Sometimes it does pay to be an Eisenhower!

A view of the first home Dwight and Mamie lived in in Gettysburg

This is the second home Dwight and Mamie rented in Gettysburg

The third home Dwight and Mamie rented in Gettysburg

Black Angus cattle on Uncle Ike's breeding farm

Breeding barn on Uncle Ike's farm in Gettysburg

The Show Barn on Uncle Ike's Gettysburg farm

Washington, D.C.

Having been to Washington D.C. several times, the most impressive to me were Arlington Cemetery, the White House, and the World War II Memorial. My first visit to Washington was in 1953 during Uncle Ike's first inauguration. Subsequent visits would take me to other parts of this great city: The Vietnam Memorial, Korean Memorial, FDR Memorial, World War II Memorial. I missed the Indian Nation Memorial due to the huge crowds on opening day and just didn't want to fight the crowds.

Arlington is a heart-rending emotional experience as I walked about and saw the graves of famous people buried there, principally John Kennedy and wife Jacqueline and the eternal flame. There were rows and rows of graves of Civil War soldiers, many unidentified. Also, there were famous Civil War officers and rows of soldiers. Watching the ceremony at the Tomb of the Unknown Soldier was moving.

Arlington is by the Metro railway stop so that anyone can visit. You don't need a car or taxi service. The Metro stops across the street from Arlington, and all you have to do is walk across the street and up the block long entry to Arlington gates. Near the gates is the Women's Memorial, principally financed by DAR (Daughters of the American Revolution) of whom several are depicted. Being a DAR member myself I was impressed by how much the DAR has done for this country, with little fanfare and recognition.

Soldiers buried at Arlington demand our utmost respect; this is an awesome place.

I visited the FDR Memorial, which stretches for acres along the tidal basin. It is a pathway through the four terms of FDR's presidency, and each section is loosely defined by granite walls and shrubbery. It is hard to tell where one section leaves off, and another begins.

The first section depicts the Great Depression. In it are statues of life-like, life-size stone figures that look very real. It is a soup line, showing the men in line waiting to get their daily ration of soup and bread. The artist made it look incredibly life-like.

Other sections show Roosevelt in his "wheeled chair" with his cloak thrown over him and chair hiding the wheels except for the two back ones. Another exhibit shows Eleanor Roosevelt in her typical cloth coat WITHOUT the ever present fox fur she always wore. Perhaps the animal rights activists clamored too much. The depiction of

Eleanor Roosevelt without her ubiquitous fox fur demeans history as it really was.

The FDR Memorial is the first presidential memorial to depict a first lady.

WORLD WAR II MEMORIAL

I visited the World War II Memorial in 2004 while visiting friends who live in Kensington. I'm glad they were with me. They knew how to get around the city. Visiting the World War II Memorial was an awesome experience, and when I saw my uncle in the center of the European Theater of Operations, it was hard to believe. Walking the site, I met many veterans. When I asked if I could take their picture by the part of the memorial that was so important to them, they were happy and pleased to let me take their pictures. They were very proud to have this memorial dedicated to them. Every citizen of this country should visit this memorial at some time.

Of all the memorials in Washington, D.C., this is the most profound.

Engraved inscription of Dwight Eisenhower's speech to his troops prior to the launch of D-Day invasion: *"You are about to embark on the great crusade toward which we have striven these many months. The eyes of the world are upon you . . . I have full confidence in your courage, devotion to duty and skill in battle."* *Dwight D. Eisenhower*

Shows the Atlantic side of the WWII Memorial

Picture of most of the Memorial with
Lincoln Memorial in the background

President Roosevelt's famous saying: the end leaves off ***"So help us God."***

OTHER STUFF

I got to see the country, every state in the union – from Maine to California, from Florida to Washington state – state parks, national parks and everything in between. I've been in every major city except New York City and Salt Lake City. Boston was my favorite place – I loved the history and how Bostonians have striven to preserve the unique history of this country and their city. Walking the Freedom Trail was a unique experience.

However, talking about all these other trips is not pertinent to the main story of my life as an Eisenhower. There are many other facets of my life. I have done many things, been many places, endured many trials.

Been there, done that! It's been a real trip, wouldn't trade it for anything.

BEHIND CLOSED DOORS

My marriage was a sham, which I kept hidden from my children and the world. My children still look back on their life as idyllic. My life was far from that, and I refuse to discuss the ugly stuff that went on. It demeans everyone.

I stayed with Tom in spite of the awfulness and abuse because I wanted the children to remember a good life. They loved their daddy. He played with them, took them for rides in the tractor. By my sticking it out, the children have wonderful memories of growing up in Illinois, their favorite place ever. Tom was a good "house husband," helping with housework and kitchen duties, primarily cleaning the stove on a regular basis. The children remember all the good stuff about him, which is good.

I finally crawled out of my marriage in 1977 a crippled person. It took me two or three years to become a real human being again, with the help of God, counseling, and determination to do what I needed to do.

I never would have traveled this road if it were not for the fact that my uncle was Dwight Eisenhower.

Many miracles followed me on my journey. I have been blessed.

THE END

Made in the USA
San Bernardino, CA
17 October 2015